The Alpha Male

The Alpha Male

A Young Man's Guide to the Big,

Wild World We Live In,

And

A Young Woman's Guide to Finding

The Real Alpha Male

John H. Ingle

SpringSource Publishing

2019

© Copyright 2019 – John H. Ingle

All rights reserved. This book is protected by the copyright laws of the United States of America. This book may not be copied or reprinted for commercial gain or profit. The use of short quotations or occasional page copying for personal or group study is permitted and encouraged. Permission will be granted upon request. Unless otherwise noted, Scripture quotations are from the NIV Study Bible Copyright © 2011 by the Zondervan Corporation. Used by permission. Scriptures marked NRSV are taken from the New Revised Standard Version Bible, copyright © 1989 National Council of the Churches of Christ in the United States of America. Used by permission. All rights reserved worldwide. Scriptures marked VOICE are taken from The Voice™. Copyright © 2012 by Ecclesia Bible Society. Used by permission. All rights reserved. Scriptures marked NKJV are taken from the New King James Version®. Copyright © 1982 by Thomas Nelson. Used by permission. All rights reserved. Any emphasis within Scripture quotations is the author's own. Pronouns used in reference to the Father, Son and Holy Spirit are capitalized throughout this book.

Cover art "Pure Passion" © 2012 by Esta Ingle, used with permission.

SpringSource Publishing, SpringSource Productions, LLC

A Texas-based Limited Liability Company, Burnet, Texas

Printed in the United States of America

Library of Congress Control Number:2019913734

ISBN-13: 978-1-7340348-0-6

Table of Contents

Chapter 1 – The Alpha Male 1
Chapter 2 – What Do Women Want? 4
Chapter 3 – Modern Woman 10
Chapter 4 – Modern Man 15
Chapter 5 – Broken and Damaged People 18
Chapter 6 – Not the Alpha Male? (Build the Man) 44
Chapter 7 – Job One is Hearing God's Voice 61
Chapter 8 – A Tale of Two Alpha Males 80
Chapter 9 – Outsourcing God 87
Chapter 10 – Unoffendable 115
Chapter 11 – Gratefulness 119
Chapter 12 – Greater Works Than These 124
Chapter 13 – Fearfully and Wonderfully Made 134
Chapter 14 – Marriage – The God Unit 147
Chapter 15 – Unity and Intimacy – The Church 164
Chapter 16 – Conscience & Who You Are 179
Chapter 17 – Your Work Life 192
Chapter 18 – Habits 199
Chapter 19 – Traveling in the Wake of Our Fathers 208
Selected Bibliography 213

Introduction

I wrote this book in the style of a personal conversation between me and other men. I want to talk to you in the same way I would if we were sitting in a coffee shop with a light rain falling, staring out the window, watching people and traffic, talking about things that don't get talked about when you're shopping, surfing the internet, or texting.

Several years back I was sweeping the garage on a spring afternoon. My youngest son, James, came by to talk. He was not quite twenty years old. I knew he had been going through a rough patch in life with career decisions and love lost. He needed some advice, and he was ready to hear it. I started talking and when I stopped a couple of hours later I had spilled out the essential principles of this book. I spoke as though I had rehearsed it all but I'd never had those specific thoughts or ideas come together before. It just poured out. I felt like I had just been given something. We had a few more conversations over the next week or so in which I elaborated on a few of the principles. Not long afterwards, he came back by the house and told me that what I had told him changed his life. He said, "Dad, you should write a book." I had to agree. This is that book. The purpose of it is not to give you a pile of rules to add to the pile of rules you already have. Life will put mountains of circumstances and choices before you. If you've received some good counsel about some of those choices already, then you might stand a better chance of making a good choice. Choices have a way of coming at you fast, with little or no warning. I want to stimulate your mind with a new way of looking at the world and your time in it. My desire for this book is that it will be good counsel. We've got a lot to cover. Let's talk.

Chapter 1 – The Alpha Male

Think of the Alpha Male in biology and the animal kingdom – you've probably seen online nature videos and television specials of the fast, aggressive male predator attacking a helpless food item, like a gazelle, sheep, or some other tasty creature. He comes in fast, with authority and strength, and shows no fear. The selected food item becomes dinner, as planned. The Alpha Male owns his territory. The lion lives in its pride. The females go out in a group to kill for the pride, but the Alpha Male lion is still the leader of the pride. Fish live in schools, and hippos and whales live in pods. Wolves live in packs. Mankind was designed to live in families. The Alpha Male, along with the accompanying female and the offspring of their union are the ingredients of the family. These units of organization are genetically built into God's design for each of them. Each of the members of the human family lives under the covering and leadership of the Alpha Male of that family unit.

When a young man which has been raised in that family has reached the age at which he is ready to take a mate, he will *"leave his father and mother and be joined to his wife, and they shall become one flesh"* (Genesis 2:24 NKJV). The family begins anew, with a newly minted Alpha Male (we hope) to lead that family unit. The Alpha Male is a leader in thought and in action. There is no Beta Male. The Beta Male is a myth and is not found within the species Homo sapiens. The mythical Beta Male is supposedly not ever able to act as an Alpha – a leader – and they must find an Alpha Male to which they attach themselves as followers. The truth is that there are Alpha Males, and not-yet-Alpha Males. God created men to become Alpha Males – every single one of them.

An unfortunate fact in our modern culture is that the term Alpha Male is mistakenly understood to refer to a patriarchal wife beater who spends the family grocery money on beer. In tandem with that notion we have created a synthetic Alpha Male replacement that is a total imposter and looks nothing like what was created back at the beginning of mankind.

Trendy magazines and websites try to sell the Alpha Male as the life of the party, drinking a particular brand of beer, handsome and smiling largely, with the girl (or girls) of his choice on his arm. He is not the Alpha Male. The Alpha Male is also not the gold chain-wearing, violence-driven drug dealer who sells lies and takes life. The real Alpha Male is not the airhead metro-sexual boy staring at you from the pages of a men's fashion magazine. The real Alpha Male is none of that. The real Alpha Male is a spiritual being that is the leader, protector of, and the provider for his family unit. He is dominant in the territory of that family unit. The Alpha Male is the man who knows who he is, who he was created to be, and is comfortable in his own skin. He knows what he wants, and why he wants it. He has a firm plan to get what he wants and needs, for himself and his family. He is guided by a sure knowledge of God and a relationship with God that prepares him for everything that's coming his way. He has gifts and talents from God that he uses to accomplish what he needs to do, for himself and his family. He fears only God. He knows that God is there

The Alpha Male

and wants, very much, to continually find and see God operating in his life. He wants to hear from God.

There is a severe shortage of Alpha Males in our world:

> *"The world is dwindling away, for lack of men; the nations are perishing for scarcity of men, for the rareness of men...Do what you will: only from God you will get men" (French Catholic Cardinal Louis Pie from his 1871 Christmas homily).*

I think the Cardinal was a pretty sharp fellow, and what he said rings true, across the boundaries and shackles of time – *"only from God will you get men."* Real men – not actors, posers, and wanna-be's. The bad news is the shortage problem in our modern culture is decidedly worse than it was in the Cardinal's day.

If you measure yourself against other men you may often either feel lacking something it seems everyone else has, or badly informed. If you feel lacking, it may be because someone has put up a better disguise than you. Men are very talented at putting up disguises – outward appearances. It's practically a national pastime. They get together in groups to test out their disguises and show them off; especially if they happen to think their current one is really effective. Some people call that male bonding, but it's usually just a chance to parade one's latest disguise – men, being peacocks.

Chapter 2 – What Do Women Want?

"The great question that has never been answered, and which I have not yet been able to answer, despite my thirty years of research into the feminine soul, is 'What does a woman want?'" - Sigmund Freud

Mr. Freud would have done well to study more about the inborn makeup of women and not so much about their outward mannerisms. Without being overly simplistic, somewhere near the top, or *at* the top of that list is that real women want an Alpha Male for their mate. They are genetically wired to seek him out and join with him. When they find him, they will usually stick with him. If they thought they found him and were fooled by his disguise, they usually won't stick around beyond that moment, because they have important life-business to tend to. If they decide to stick around anyway, it may be because they have ulterior motives that keep them there until that motive is satisfied or no longer exists. If she feels too financially vulnerable or has too many other distractions or threats in her life, she may put off leaving. A wise woman may also choose a man based on what she sees his potential to be, confident in his ability to grow into an Alpha Male. But, ultimately, if she's not with you as her Alpha Male, or soon-to-be Alpha Male, she is already gone – you're just waiting for the news. If she's forced to stay, there is a serious penalty to be paid for holding her there.

The Alpha Male

Women feel secure with an Alpha Male. When big, bad things hit the fan, and life seems suddenly very cheap, and very temporary, a woman immediately turns to look for her Alpha Male. Her deep-seated genetically-wired desire is that she already knows where to find him, and that *he's already coming to find her.* She is looking for cover because her DNA has wired her to survive and look after the survival of their offspring, whether born yet, or ensconced within the eggs she has carried since before she was born. She has biological imperatives that are so seriously stamped into her DNA that you mess with those imperatives at your own peril. When Sarah Palin talked about not messing with mama grizzlies, she wasn't trying to be cute – she was trying to introduce you to a powerful concept through a metaphor – a word picture. I don't know of anything more dangerous than a fully formed mother protecting her young. Just so you know, the capacity is in there, you just may not have witnessed it yet. If you're very fortunate, you'll never see it. God made them that way, so don't try to put some blame-thing on them for it. She is wired to seek out security and survival for her family. She is blessed with innate talents to do that and do it well.

But, women are more inclined to value safety than men. Women are not so well known for having said:

"Hey, let's:

'…set sail, anyway, that storm doesn't look too bad;'

'…ride that bull – it looks like fun;'

'…jump out of that airplane into the enemy's backyard;'

'…catch that snake, and see if it's poisonous,'" and so on.

John H. Ingle

Given that a lot men have died doing things like that, it seems reasonable to consider that women may even be more intelligent in that regard. Their DNA isn't quite so wired for that sort of view of life. Women generally don't volunteer for facing death by knife fight in wartime, because it's not the way they're wired. Dying in a door-to-door gun battle means that the potential life within her also dies. Even in highly unusual national circumstances, such as in the Israeli Defense Forces, only a few percent of the women serving operate in some capacity that puts them near the front lines. But, they are not deployed in a manner that would deliberately expose them to combat.

A woman serving on the front lines in hand-to-hand combat is a raw contradiction in DNA wiring and physical design that is an awful error, meant only to gain political points for its philosophical followers in a fallen world. Imagine yourself for a moment: you're in a running gun battle trying to reach the helicopter extraction zone, hundreds of yards away. You're being pursued by angry warriors of similar skill, armed with serious automatic weapons. Your teammate is a female and you're both in Special Operations. You are suddenly wounded and unable to run or walk. You weigh 185 pounds and she weighs 140. The only way you'll both survive is if she carries you that last two hundred yards, while firing her weapon effectively. Your weight is in addition to the seventy pounds of gear already strapped to her body. You're probably both going to die. It's just physics, not politics.

Women are tuned for survival and security but with a totally different approach than men. However, the goal of their kind of security is not the most valuable trait for keeping the family free from domination, destruction, or slavery by outside forces. The inborn traits of the Alpha Male are much better suited for providing and maintaining that freedom in a sometimes violent world. It isn't a value judgment. It doesn't mean he is a superior creation for having that response built into his DNA. It just means he's not a girl. They really are different and every day I'm glad for that.

What a woman is genetically wired to seek from a man – just like a magnet to steel – is relationship, provision, and protection. Love combined with respect is the glue that holds that relationship together. Women – much more often than men – may use a "love" relationship or accelerated marriage as a means to escape a bad home situation. Escape from an undesirable living situation is all too often the mechanism that promotes a relationship between a male and female. Both men and women are all too capable of using that imaginary way out. But, it is a bad choice. If he's NOT the Alpha Male and the assurance of provision and protection are not there, defended by respect and love, then the female is made to feel that no one has her back and she's still looking for the real Alpha Male. She is almost coldly practical about the role of the Alpha Male – usually more so than the Alpha Male, himself. But, she is far more likely to tolerate an Alpha Male in a relationship without love than she will a "love" relationship with someone who is not really a true Alpha Male.

In speaking of Abraham's wife, Sarah, we're told that:

> *"You are her daughters if you do what is right and do not give way to fear (1 Peter 3:6)."*

Fear of what? Fear of the loss of provision and protection. That threat of loss may not be happening now, when it's a sunny day, and the winds and sea are calm. But, it can happen on that bad day that seems bound to come around more than once in life.

John H. Ingle

Self-Worth – or – Who's Your Daddy?

The Alpha Male lives in freedom and security – he is secure in who he is, in who God is, and what his relationship is to God. The Alpha Male is secure because God is secure. The Alpha Male's Daddy is secure.

In the Bible we see:

> *"Husbands love your wives, just as Christ loved the church and gave himself up for her..." (Ephesians 5:25).*

Why was Christ giving himself up for the Church? He was doing that for its provision and its protection – he was willing to – and did – die for it. His provision was salvation and healing through His eternal sacrifice that brings forgiveness through repentance. Christ's protection was in sending the Holy Spirit as our companion – that still, small voice that we need to be hearing so often – the awesome voice of God. Every time we celebrate the Lord's Supper we openly acknowledge that provision and protection. The wife needs to know that the husband's commitment to her is so strong that he would die to insure that her provision and protection would endure – just as Jesus did.

Jesus is the ultimate Alpha Male.

I recommend that you measure yourself against Jesus, the earthly image of the Father in Heaven, "in whom there is no shadow of turning." He loves you so much. He wants you to know who your Daddy is. Recall, if you can, lyrics from an old Bob Dylan tune, *"you're gonna serve somebody."* In life, there are two choices; serve God, or reject Him and serve the dark forces of evil, even if you don't know you're doing that. You will ultimately do one or the other, whether you like it or not. All the atheists I've ever met worship and serve themselves, thinking that there really couldn't be anyone smarter or more sophisticated than they are. Unwittingly, they have joined Satan in his declaration that:

> *"I will ascend into heaven, I will exalt my throne above the stars of God: I will sit also upon the mount of the congregation, in the sides of the north: I will ascend above the heights of the clouds; I will be like the most High"* (Isaiah 14:12).

Perhaps without fully realizing it, those poor misguided souls who have rejected God have joined their hope with that of Satan – that if they wish, plot and plan thoroughly enough, they will replace God with themselves. This is a very bad choice. You won't make a very good god on your own. So, that should settle one matter – who you're going to serve in life. The other is whether or not you'll enjoy it, both now and later.

Truly deciding to serve God leads to uncorking that deep-seated need to get to know Him, better. That deep-seated need is already there, you just might not have figured out what it's about. Along the way, man discovers woman, also. That becomes another deep-seated need that needs a lot of understanding. Let's start finding out more about both.

Chapter 3 – Modern Woman

The Destruction of Modern Woman

"Choice." It's a big word. When Cain slew Abel it was "choice." It was an awful and permanently destructive choice. That choice was so bad that Cain told God that, "My guilt is too great to bear." In many translations it says, "My punishment…" but the original Hebrew – *avon* – is better translated as "guilt." His sin of purposefully taking his brother's life in his moment of anger was so intolerable and unacceptable to the rest of God's Creation that he feared for his life. God placed on him a "mark" so that anyone who thought to take vengeance on him for his awful crime would know that Cain was not to be touched.

The "Modern World" would like for you to approach the murder of your unborn child as a very wholesome lifestyle choice. This imaginary world approves of aborting one's child, if for no other reason than to celebrate one's "mastery" of themselves – a show of independence. But, what an awful place to be, for a woman who has committed such a grievous sin – a sin so great that it is specifically called out in the Ten Commandments – "Thou shall not murder." Yet, here she is, murdering her own offspring in the name of convenience and a pseudo-spiritual statement of her power and authority; the same offspring that is so strongly embedded in her DNA to protect at any cost. With her child dead, she finds herself greatly wounded, with her guilt "too great to bear." She will now urgently pursue an emotional defense for committing this grievous act and is rewarded with modern culture's warm, protective embrace that she's just exercising her "rights" as a real woman. She should be proud. What a staggering contrast and shift of values – from murderer to cultural role model. Countless women have found themselves in years of counseling, seeking relief from the awful guilt of having had an abortion. Some of them bury the guilt so deeply that their crumbling lives don't even remember the reason for their self-hatred. It's both startling and bewildering to consider that women can be convinced and be activated to empathize with all sorts of bizarre "social justice" causes, but then not have enough empathy for their unborn child to spare its life. Meanwhile, women who have not had an abortion and probably never would are drawn in empathy to the side of their suffering sister. Their empathy for the suffering sister they can see overrides the empathy for the dead child, whom they cannot see.

> *"It is a poverty to decide that a child must die so that you may live as you wish." - - Mother Theresa*

And poverty it is, and we're *not* talking about money. The suffering for many women is more than they can freely admit, particularly since the "Modern World" wants to bestow a medal upon her for her horrendous act. But, the modern women's movement is busy finding them other, more important matters to attend to – job equality, pay equality, gender equality of…what? What is it that is supposed to be equal? It's not an injustice that men and women are not equal – God never intended for them to be equal. He intended for them to be harmonious – aptly fit to become *one* in His eyes – **unified**. Women, suffering with that deep soul pain that comes with taking the life of their child, are steered towards "modern woman." There she is encouraged to mask her guilt and fear with the righteous badge of the Social Justice Warrior. She now has a cause to ease her pain. The Warrior screams they should be just like men, with the assumption that men somehow are having all the fun and have all the authority. If men have all the authority – that is, ultimate, primal authority over the heavens and the earth, then what does God have? The easy answer is that men don't have all the authority. They have only the authority God gives them. Authority is not a bed of roses, and it's not necessarily fun.

Women who have had an abortion and are sucked into this modern self-absorbed culture stew find themselves not wanting to be themselves – they want to be somebody else – someone who doesn't have this awful ache inside. For all this there has always been only one cure – the same cure it always is – repentance before the One who created both them and their baby. Repentance can come when a woman realizes the horror that she has embraced in killing the life growing within her – THE number one task that God has firmly planted into her genetic structure and her soul. The horror now testifies against her, and is a continual reminder of her guilt. It is, once more, that the unborn child's *"blood cries out to me from the ground!"* (Genesis 4:10).

Repentance brings God's forgiveness, and forgiveness brings the opportunity for healing and restoration. However, becoming involved with a woman in that state of mind prior to her repentance and restoration is a scary move and one that should be studiously avoided. After restoration has a firm footing, she may be able to enter into a relationship with her heart and soul in the right place, but it is a dangerous place for a man to be until then. Her heart, her mind, and her life are going to change. You should give her the time and space to do that.

The Alpha Male

Un-Natural Woman

It's obvious to any mature Christian that women are exactly who God made them to be, and they: aren't cattle; aren't without personal rights (at least in the U.S.); aren't commodities or property, and aren't disposable. They *are* God's precious gift to man. The story of man without woman would have been over a very long time ago.

As a modern young woman seeks out someone that she thinks looks like an Alpha Male, she is surprised to find that there are very few of them around. There may be none at all that she can see in or near her life that are similar in age. There are plenty of pretenders. The male that she does find may not even make a good placeholder. The modern culture has been extremely effective at emasculating young men. Meanwhile, young Alpha Males who have fought off emasculation are searching for potential brides and are finding young women who are trying to be Alpha Males. They don't look like potential brides to young Alpha Males. They look like trouble. Modern woman, stewing in this bizarre Hollywood culture, whether completely separated from God or not, now feels compelled to *become* the Alpha Male. She does have a strong desire to survive. What other choice does she have? But, once she can presume the righteous authority to murder the life within, she can be manipulated to assume any authority – even authority that makes no sense and lies way outside the way we were created. This internal emotional struggle for authority is encouraged by dark powers. Young women are told that they have now become morally superior and that she should seize this authority and become a champion of the modern culture. If men are incapable of leading – then the woman must lead. These damaged women invest themselves in encouraging other women to take the same dark leap they took. Misery does, indeed, love company. With the help of a governmental bureaucracy that is happy to do just about anything for votes, and the darkness of evil beckoning on every side, it's easy to assume that authority. Women are cheered for stepping into that oozing swamp of deception to drown their lives and the lives of their intended families.

So, what *should* be happening in the lives of women? For starters, as they grow up, they should be getting the training needed by all young women that prepares them to become the bride of a real Alpha Male. They should also be taught to correctly recognize the Alpha Male, and not be fooled by all of the posing, bragging and strutting, as they will see plenty of it. They need to be taught the roles of jobs, business, and money. The craving for money and position can confuse women just as easily as it does men. A mother's job is to provide that training – to identify the Alpha Male for the daughters and to identify and expose the imitation. The father's job is to validate that training by BEING the Alpha Male, in a strong, loving relationship with those daughters, demonstrating protection, provision, and wisdom. He has a big example to set. In addition, the young woman should be seeing her parents in a strong, loving relationship that puts their relationship with God right in the middle of it. The problem in modern society is that these skills and values have been so damaged and devalued that they are an endangered species. Instead, children are being raised by Hollywood, social media and their closest clueless friends. But, before we go further along that path, let's look at Modern Man.

Chapter 4 – Modern Man

The Assault on the Alpha Male

The popular modern culture has been waging continual war on the Alpha Males of the world, particularly in the Western world. It is a beat-down. It has been going on for several decades and has been extremely effective. It has been said that television is a reflection of the society around us. Look at some of the male figures on TV over the last couple of generations. The '70's television character, Archie Bunker, was a complete windbag, idiot, bigot, and racist who could hardly put two kind words together for anyone. His wife was a ditzy, hand-wringing worrier who had much more superior feelings and is, therefore, a good person. Archie is not a good person but he is a father and husband. Even if he said something halfway sensible, we were still supposed to hate him.

The average father on TV is a buffoon. Peter Griffin of the current day Family Guy series is another real winner. His self-centered life leaves no room for anyone else and his ability to comprehend what anyone else needs or wants is non-existent. He treats his wife and children as objects that decorate his life whenever it's convenient. He neglects them or sacrifices them to get what he wants on a regular basis. Even though he is a comedic parody of sorts, that fact may be largely lost on his fans. He is immensely popular as a cartoon comedian. But, he is the anti-Alpha Male – the very opposite of what the Alpha Male is. Characters like Archie and Peter are successful tools for tearing down what being a husband and father looks like if that's all you have to go on. For an awfully large number of American families, the crucial values of life are being taught by vampire movies, internet music videos, and school hallway gossip.

Modern Man: he's an idiot…a bumbler…helpless…weak…lost. People put up with him because that's the kindest thing to do with the jerk. It's illegal to murder him – at least for now. We're not even sure why we keep him around. He's a lot of trouble to clean up after. What a disturbing figure – especially as a template for young men to measure themselves against, and try to figure out what values he brings for them to emulate in their own lives. There are no positives – only negatives.

The popular culture is currently being dosed with a message about "toxic masculinity." It's very likely that you could find an institution of "higher learning" that would offer you a Master's or PhD in "Toxic Masculinity Studies." Such is the extent to which we have organized and promoted our mental illnesses and our departure from God's designed destination. Masculinity is not toxic. Sin is toxic. The author Neil Postman once said that children are our message to the future. Christians are to be living as God's message to the present, carrying His Word and His message to a depraved, lost, and burning world that will ultimately be totally destroyed – to the point that the very elements will be consumed.

The end goal of the war against the Alpha Male is to reduce all men to a state of need and dependency on external authority. In the near term, dependency on schools, the government and its ruling elite will pave the way. Ultimately, the accuser, HaSatan, will assert itself as the real puppet-master behind the scenes. Alpha Males are not dependency-oriented, so they have been identified as enemies of those who are striving for that nightmarish future. Make no mistake – the evil one is the driving force behind all of this. He may use gullible and needy people, and certainly he will use those who willingly and knowingly enable him, to accomplish his goals. But, the people pushing this agenda are just throwaway pawns in his world. The former Communist dictator Josef Stalin called them "useful idiots." These are people who have been deceived in a way that prevents them from seeing and understanding truth. These are people who reject God and even think they can defeat Him. Publicly debating and arguing against these individuals may momentarily seem like good sport if you can score a public victory. But, it is largely ineffective, temporary and pretty much a grand waste of your time and resources. Rational discussion doesn't seem to have much effect anymore in this "modern" culture.

Chapter 5 – Broken and Damaged People

Childhood Dreams and Car Wrecks Along the Way

I wasn't afraid of much as a boy. I already had my Dad for that. He was pretty much the scariest person I had ever known or met when I was a young guy. My Dad was the son of a Baptist preacher. He joined the Army Reserves when he was a teenager and was apprenticing to be an electrician. The second big war in Europe and the Pacific had started and suddenly he was a foot soldier about to ship out of a snowbound training camp in Massachusetts to some hellhole in Europe. He saw a poster in one of the training rooms that said he could take a test to become a pilot. He signed up for the test and passed with flying colors. He was immediately issued new orders to report for pilot training, instead of shipping out for the ground war in Europe the following week.

Quite a few months later, he flew his brand new four-engine B24G Liberator bomber out of Southern California, headed for the war zone in the South Pacific. On his collars sat the brass-colored bars of a 2nd Lieutenant. In the Pacific he would bomb enemy positions, and he and his crew would do relentless combat with enemy fighter planes for the right to return to home base alive that day. We never spoke of the war

The Alpha Male

when I was a younger man. My mother said that she didn't get her husband back after the war. She got this person. And, he was angry...really angry. That's the part I remember...the anger. There weren't many days when I didn't see some reminder of that anger. None of my friends came to my house, as in *none*. They were petrified at the thought of being in the same room with him and would crawl across broken glass to avoid it. All I knew was that I needed to get out on my own as soon as it was humanly possible and not live there, ever again. I also knew that I didn't want to be anything like him. Someday, I'd have kids and they would love me and I would love them, and my wife would be sunny and smiling, and make my life joyous and complete.

Around the age of nine, several bouts with rheumatic fever delayed my body's normal rate of development. My joints swelled and ached. To avoid permanent damage to them, I had to lie still in bed for 24 hours a day for months on end. I wasn't permitted to sit up in bed without someone helping me. I was carried to the bathroom. I consumed a lot of penicillin and a lot of buffered aspirin. I had blood draws every week and felt like a human pin cushion. There was very little to do besides read, so I became a serial reader. I read everything anyone would bring me. I read the entire Encyclopedia Britannica. Much of it I really didn't understand because I didn't yet have the historical context needed to make real sense of things like geo-politics, race and ethnicity, and wars. I liked the pictures a lot and dreamed of a life that didn't include lying in a bed. I read the Bible at least twice. I read the Book of Knowledge set of encyclopedias. The world was a lot larger to me than the little bedroom that was my world. I had "home-bound teachers" that visited me a couple of times per week and tried to keep me up with traditional schooling, but my intensive reading put me academically ahead of most of my peers. By the fifth grade I was testing at the college level in reading comprehension. My social skills withered and lay dormant.

About six months after I was confined to bed, while seeming to be almost recovered, I experienced what I believe was my first miracle. On my ankle, a dime-sized, round spot was turning red, was hot and the bone itself seemed to be softening and it was very sore. Most doctors did house calls in those days, especially mine. He often brought more doctors with him so that they could see first-hand what the symptoms of rheumatic fever looked like, as the condition was fairly rare. He stopped by the house on his way to another emergency and took a quick look. I remember his conversation with my mother. He wasn't sure. One of the phrases that he uttered was "osteomyelitis." At that I saw my mom's face move from concern to dread, and I realized that this could be the beginning of something really bad. The doctor told her to bring me to his office the next morning. That night I prayed most of the night, asking the Lord to heal me. The next morning all the symptoms were gone. There was no pain, no redness, no softness, no hot skin – nothing. I knew that the Lord had intervened on my behalf.

At the age of ten I had to learn to walk, all over again. It was bizarre. My brain knew things that my body no longer did. I went into relapse twice more before I escaped it all. My second miracle was that I had survived 3 bouts with rheumatic fever and had no obvious heart damage. Recovery was slow. At 12, I could make it about halfway around a 440 yard cinder track before passing out. I was chased or beat up on the way home from school one or two days per week through middle school and learned what it was like to be the butt of the joke. I walked to church every Sunday for Sunday School and church service. I was back again Wednesday evening for Prayer Meeting and choir practice. At the invitation of my Sunday School teacher I had already

The Alpha Male

given my life to Jesus. I read the Bible. A lot. I began to make some good friends at Southside Baptist Church – people that seemed to love me and treated me like they would want to see me again. It was some shelter from the storm that was my home.

Back at school my teachers were pretty nice to me, especially my English teacher. She liked words and puns and fun ways to manipulate the language for a good time. So did I. I liked her a lot and she liked me. I also learned how to insult someone without them being sure whether I had, or not. I learned that words could be a weapon. I also discovered that I could be very funny, using clever words. I became the class wise-guy in just about every class. I could even make my teachers laugh, along with the rest of the class. It would be quite a few years before I would discover the life-altering activity of speaking God's blessing into a life.

Life was getting better, but then, each day, there was that moment when I had to leave all that fun and cross into the danger zone of Physical Education (PE). There, I was sickly and puny and the coaches, of all people, seemed to have no reservations about making fun of me. I think they thought I had chosen this lifestyle, and that I needed badgering so I would shape up. One of my coaches was a Sunday School teacher at a different Baptist church. He had more fun names to call me. He didn't act like any of my Sunday School teachers, so I tried to avoid him. PE was a bad and dangerous place to be.

Meanwhile, I learned how to read my Dad pretty effectively. When he was having a really bad day I could blend into the paint on the wall. My sisters apparently didn't have that ability and paid heavily for it. My mom would sometimes refer to me privately as The Negotiator. I seemed to have a way of getting past his worst. I just understood it as survival – a way to keep me alive until I could bail out. The Corpus

John H. Ingle

Christi Naval Air Station closed their Overhaul and Repair facility where my dad worked on avionics and aircraft wiring. Thousands lost their jobs. Corpus Christi, Texas plunged into a never-ending recession and there were no good jobs. Odd jobs, low-skill part time jobs, help from friends and family – which my Dad always hated accepting – kept us from losing the house and starving. I stayed away from my Dad as much as possible. He seemed to be even angrier, lately.

I went out for basketball in the ninth grade, intent upon regaining my physical health. I was the second shortest guy on the team and had the biggest feet. The coach had to special order my shoes. He said they looked like swimming flippers, so he called me Flipper, after a porpoise on a popular TV show of the day. That was an improvement over his previous nickname for me. My body finally began to grow. I collected some automotive engine flywheels that I used as training weights and I worked out in the garage just about every night. I swore to myself that there would come a day when no one would be beating me up on my way home from school, anymore.

Things had seemed to get a little better when my Dad went back to flying. He started teaching flying night classes and rejoined the Air Force through the Texas Air National Guard (ANG) as a multi-engine pilot, flying the fighter group's C47. He finally overcame his hatred of flying as a great way to die that day. But, he had a sort of gallows sense of humor. He told me a one-liner pilot joke one day. "When an engine fails on a twin-engine airplane you always have enough power left to get you to the crash site." In those days he usually flew a twin-engine plane. His humor was a bit on the edgy side. But, then he also got a job as an air traffic controller – the exact opposite job of what was needed for someone with stress and anger issues. It's considered to be one of the most high stress jobs you can do. He became even more tightly wound, which was really saying something. My two older sisters got out as fast as they could, and *pffft*, they were gone – mentally battered, bruised, and damaged, but also gone.

I started to make more friends at school but I was pretty shy inside from the years of being bullied. I could act more sociable than I really was. Middle school kids are the meanest in the world. Either you are the jokester or the butt of the joke – there is no in-between. If there is any point in a kid's life when home-schooling could be really important, it is in those years. For boys in middle school the focus is on "like me" or "other." Our DNA wires us to seek "like me" and to avoid "other," as a survival technique. "Like me" means they look sort of like me, they talk sort of like me and they act sort of like me. They're also prepared to fight back like me, and they will. "Other" means they don't look like me, they don't act like me, and they may or may not fight back. This sociological phenomenon is a scientific fact, like it or not. But, middle school boys take that to an extreme in the squabbling for bragging rights and are always ready to punish "other" for even being seen in the same location as "like me." At that point in my life, I was still "other," due largely to the socialization gap from being sick and out of school for so long. But I was still good at surviving and I was determined to make a go of it. I had to get a job. I knew that it would help my self-image if I could dress nicely for school. Then, if I couldn't actually *speak* to a girl, maybe she would speak to me. What would happen then, I had no idea.

I soon found a job at the public library as a Librarian's Page, and worked my way up, over several years, to being the Reference Librarian's Assistant. In those days, there were no computers, no search engine, and no internet. There was a public library with a reference section and most of the public could not even go into that shelf area. Most books there couldn't even be checked out but could be used in the reading room under the watchful eye of the staff. If you had a difficult question to answer, like "How many metric tons of wheat were produced in the Ukraine last year?" you could ask the Reference Librarian for help finding the answer. I was forever curious and still reading a couple of books per week so it was about my favorite job, ever. I worked nights and weekends and I eventually even drove the Bookmobile.

In high school I began to run with a bit rougher crowd – not criminals or nasty people – but people you didn't mess with unless you just weren't very smart. One of them, who became a good friend, fought open class Golden Gloves boxing and did very well. He was also very adept at martial arts. I was the court jester and they were my protection – my guardians. Nobody messed with us – not even the jocks, who carefully and respectfully avoided us. Finally, there was that sense of personal security – safety – that had seemed so elusive thus far in life. I had a home – even if only for a short time.

My Dad found it pretty difficult to express love. He would laugh sometimes – the kind of laugh that has a cynical, hard edge to it that reminded you that it wasn't really humorous, just hard, like stone. I'm not really sure what he ever thought was fun. Many years later, most of my extended family of cousins would admit that they were scared spit-less of him, and stayed as far away from him as they could. But, I was the oldest son, and he had a complete plan mapped out for my life.

His plan was that as soon as I finished my senior year in high school I would join the Air Force through the Texas Air National Guard. I had done my research and told him that I was automatically classified 4F, or physically unfit for duty, due to my multiple bouts of rheumatic fever. He looked at me like I'd just hand-strangled the family dog and asked, "What are you…a chickenshit?" Well, obviously that was not

The Alpha Male

the case so, as Marty McFly of "Back to the Future" would have done, I joined the Guard, and neglected to mention my medical issues. I was a Weapons Control Systems Specialist. I worked on F102A Delta Dagger fighter jets at Kelly Air Force Base that carried nuclear-tipped missiles and scrambled to UFO reports over the southern U.S. border. We considered ourselves to be the "tip of the spear" in the defense of our national airspace.

The emotional pain I had been raised with was more powerful in my life than a "calling" on my life. I knew a lot more about what I *didn't* want to be than what I *did* want to be. I had opportunities but I had no understanding of how to steer my life to use my real talents so, instead, I used skills I gained in the process along the way.

The electronics and logic state training I gained in the Air Force was pretty intense. "Black box" fighter jets with interchangeable components were starting to come online, but I was working with older fighters that used a lot of resistors, diodes, transistors, capacitors and coils, all neatly soldered individually onto single-layer circuit boards. The schematic manuals for my bird, when stacked, were over a foot tall. They had to train us in the details – lots of details. They were complex in the extreme. We would track down the problems, get a solder gun and actually replace individual electronic components – not just swap out a replaceable plug-in module and throw the old one away.

Electronics was something I *could* do, not something I was *called* to do. With better training as a young man I would have been made aware that I needed to hear God's voice in my life and He would guide me in these life choices. I kept thinking I wanted to be a doctor, but I had an aversion to hospitals and places where I might catch something and find myself back in bed, again. Sunday School and Church were about getting people saved, not oriented towards learning to have an active relationship with the one, true God, who would actually talk to you. God talking to you would get you a bed with guards at the doors and bars on the windows. Training young men in the days of my youth was something that was rather badly done, if at all. Training was mostly about how to behave – very much Ten Commandments oriented.

Today, the training provided to most young men is horrendously done by social media and peer pressure, and they're exposed to more garbage than ever. Their female counterparts are no better off. Both young men and young women in their teen years are typically not getting anything close to what they need to prepare them for the storm waiting for them, outside. As a result, bad things can, and often do, happen.

After a couple of tours of active duty I found myself back in college in Corpus Christi. I lived in the dorm on campus. All those years of suppressed life and emotion seemed to come popping out in spades. Bad behavior, or at least inadvisable behavior, seemed to be my frequent companion, along with doing just enough school to stay off scholastic probation most of the time. I found love for the first time. It seemed mutual and I began to make life plans of my own, but they were pretty grainy and out-of-focus. I had been dating the same girl for about a year and a half and I was pretty sure it would end in marriage. One night we were at a very rowdy party and we both had too much to drink. We were outside in her car and she suddenly bolted from the car and ran off down an alley. I chased her through alleys and across parking lots. When I caught her she was inconsolable and sobbing. "What are we doing here? Why are we here? What's it all about?" I was speechless. A lot of things ran through my mind in a big hurry. If I told her the truth, then suddenly my current life would testify against me and my wayward state. The alternative was that I could try

The Alpha Male

to recover where I had been years earlier. We could both join a church and we could become "church-people – nice people." We could leave our children in the nursery during church. We could go to picnics. Baptist picnics had awesome potato salad and killer fried chicken, and we would be "good people." It wasn't enough to keep me there the last time and I knew it would not keep me there this time. I had no words of wisdom for her. My understanding of God's love at this point was mostly wrapped around His wrath and possible ways of avoiding it. My image of the Heavenly Father – The Master of The Universe – was still tied too closely to the image of my earthly father and the pain that it represented. The fact that I would need for the Lord to be a central part of my marriage to a woman was not an idea that had yet taken hold in me, regardless of what anyone might have said in Sunday School.

God had placed a deep-seated need within me for a spiritual awareness of the world, but I saw no pathway for living it. So, I had pushed it down until I couldn't see it anymore beneath the cares of the world. I don't remember much about the rest of our conversation in that alley but I wasn't being honest with her or myself. Things slowly changed between us in ways I didn't quite understand. My behavior didn't really improve. Suddenly, first love was lost as I was changing schools to the University of Texas, and I was devastated. I didn't understand what the Alpha Male was, yet, or what it meant, but at that moment in time I was not one. She knew she wasn't protected, and provision for a family was even more uncertain. I did not have her back. I didn't know what I was or wasn't. But, I was completely beat down. I had transferred with a major in Chemistry and found myself so unable to think or concentrate that I decided I had to have a mission – something that would energize me with meaning and order. I had to change paths.

John H. Ingle

At the time, I was actively anti-war – this was the middle of the Vietnam buildup into a major conflict, and a stack of government lies that seemed to have no end. When you're on the inside you hear a lot of the talk that never makes it onto the television. My anti-war positions were very vocal and it often didn't sit well back in my Guard unit where I was still serving out my six year stint at the rank of Sargent. I decided Journalism and Sociology were a much better fit for my distressed and battered psyche and I moved over to the UT School of Journalism, where I could wage war against the tyranny of centralized abused power. That worked for a little while, but slowly the wheels began to fall off. Survival wasn't working anymore. I wasn't surviving. I was dead broke and I was losing my motivation to do anything, but I also had no desire to starve. I was no longer studying depersonalization in a classroom, I was living it.

I dragged myself into Strait Music Company, a few blocks from my cheap, hippie crashpad in central Austin, where Mike Thorpe, a friend from my ANG unit managed the guitar and amp department. I told him my tale of despair and he said I should start repairing guitars and amps for the store. He said they had to send them out to a radio and TV repair shop and those guys didn't understand the issues – a guitar amp was not a TV. It sounded better than hunger and homelessness, so I accepted the offer. I played guitar, so I would at least be working in an area of familiarity.

They gave me a small area in one of their south Austin warehouses to set up a workshop and start working. Wizard Electronics was born and work went well. More and more musicians would hunt me down and beg me to fix their sound systems or guitars, electric pianos, and so on. I was pretty much the only game in town. I could get on the guest list at any live music club in town and get at least my first drink for free. If something stopped working while I was there I was sort of an EMS

The Alpha Male

for band equipment. I even fixed B.B. King's guitar, affectionately known as Lucille, one night before a show. Life seemed to be taking a turn for the better.

One of my regular customers was guitarist John Staehely, at that time of the legendary Texas boogie band, Krackerjack. His brother, Al, had recently replaced Mark Andes on bass in the West Coast band Spirit. Spirit was one of the seminal West Coast bands in the same era as The Jefferson Airplane and Buffalo Springfield. Mark and Jay Ferguson had left Spirit to help form the new band, Jo Jo Gunne. Spirit's guitarist, Randy California, had suffered a head injury in a horse riding accident and didn't want to tour anymore so John Locke, Ed Cassidy and Al wanted John to come to Malibu and audition as guitarist. John came back from the audition and asked if I wanted to go on the road with them. I was ready for something bigger and more exciting, so I wrapped up my affairs in Austin and we hit the road several weeks later.

Southern California was so different from Austin that it took a bit to get my social bearings. The job was to be drum roadie for Ed Cassidy, guitar roadie for John, and sound mixer out front at the console during the concert. My new friend and road-mate, John Hunt, took care of setting up the grand piano, the bass guitar rig, and managing the stage.

All of that concert touring slowly began to include recording studio experience and I was able to persuade an apprenticeship of sorts working under Alex Kazanegras. Alex worked with Loggins and Messina, Janis Joplin, Sly Stone and many other big name artists, and he was now working with Spirit Featuring the Staehely Brothers. Alex and his partner, John Fiore, had Haji Sound's mobile recording studio backed up to their office back door at Crossroads of the World in Hollywood. I started reading my Bible, again. It had been a while, but the deep-seated need for spiritual connection had reawakened. These were heady times of hotels, airports, truck rentals, equipment setups and tear-downs, trips to foreign countries and to states that almost seemed like foreign countries. I really didn't have much of a personal life. I wouldn't go out with a girl that I wouldn't consider marrying, and in Southern California that list seemed to remain extremely short. I met lots of party girls but it was rare to meet someone with whom I would consider a personal relationship. My personal life was mostly in a deepfreeze while daily life was mostly about building a career.

I had been roommates for a while with Spirit's bass player, Al Staehely (aka – "The Rock & Roll Lawyer") and then, later on, with my road-mate and good friend, John Hunt. Spirit had morphed into the Staehely Brothers. The Staehely Brothers brought in drummer Cozy Powell, formerly of the Jeff Beck Group, and John Locke came back on keyboards. They were phenomenal and the record companies were suddenly very interested in our health and our future. It seemed that superstardom was in the wings and ready to take flight. Shortly after their very first US tour, Cozy's girlfriend decided she didn't like California and told Cozy to pack – they're going back to England. It felt like a hard left turn into the very cold Pacific Ocean.

All the while I had maintained a friendship with Spirit pianist John Locke. We often spent late evenings discussing philosophy and the world of the spirit. One night while we were discussing Astral Projection he warned me that this was a very strange place to go and things could get very dicey out there. I wasn't sure exactly what he meant by that but I pressed ahead. I knew that there was much more to the world than what we could see with our eyes; something noteworthy, something that was even exciting. I was determined to find out more about it.

The Alpha Male

For many years most of the Church has been avoiding the discussion of the spiritual world and how it might be a bit more radical than you can imagine. If you believe the Bible, God has been doing some pretty radical things for thousands of years, yet we act like that's all over – done. Everything now became a Sunday Picnic & Social – calm, sedate, no surprises – plenty of potato salad and fried chicken for everyone. The problem was I knew there was something there but I couldn't find it in the Church. I was pretty intent upon finding it. The giant boulder of a fact is that our young men will see visions and our old men will dream dreams, and if they're willing, they *will* hear from God. We can hide and pretend it's not real, but then what? If the Church can't deal with the real world then Christians will ignore the organized Church and try to find their own way, often to be led astray, and become largely ineffective at doing what we're supposed to be doing.

I had been studying extra-sensory perception (ESP) for quite a few years. I was looking for an explanation and understanding of certain spiritual events that had happened in my life. I had "seen" events before they happened. I sometimes "knew things" that I had no way of knowing. I couldn't control it and didn't know why I was experiencing these things. I had read widely on the subject to find what others in the world of science and the paranormal had to say. I had read much of what Dr. John Lilly had published, such as *The Mind of the Dolphin*, *Programming and Metaprogramming in the Human Biocomputer*, and *The Center of the Cyclone*. Much of Lilly's work had involved reaching spiritual pathways through either sensory deprivation (isolation tanks) or through the conduit of hallucinogenic substances. But, I was more interested in reaching there without any outside help that might distort the reality and understanding of it.

John H. Ingle

I began to systematically explore the world of the spirit and of projection – that out-of-body experience that one goes into purposefully and willingly to visit a different place outside space and time. I knew that there were parlor tricks and there was real. I was not at all interested in parlor tricks. I wanted the real. I began to discover a world I'd never seen before – a world you could see without eyes. One late night I was experimenting in meditation and suddenly I became starkly aware of an evil, the likes of which I had never imagined coming up alongside me. I knew, instinctively, that this strange entity was there for no good purpose. It began to whisper, telling me that I was all alone, lost in the darkest recesses of space, and that the "reality" I thought I knew was an elaborate hoax – a construction of my mind, meant to keep me from realizing my hopeless state. The only way out was to end it, which would happen someday anyway, without all that needless suffering in the meantime. The evil was correct in assuring me that I was alone. I had ventured into territory wherein I had no knowledge or understanding and had gone there without the covering of the Lord. I had strayed far from the camp and my defenses were down. I recoiled in stark horror. Suddenly, it felt as if I really was tumbling through space and then I re-entered a conscious state in my bed, in a cold sweat, with my pulse pounding. I knew that I had just experienced a very close brush with death and decided that this was not a benign pursuit and was not something I wanted to repeat. I decided not to pursue that dark alley into the supernatural.

Several weeks after that I was asked to come on board with Jo Jo Gunne and we began touring. Our second time out would include England. That tour would become "the tour from Hell." Everything that could go wrong did go wrong. I was used to very tight, professional touring with minimal stress and even some fun mixed in.

The Alpha Male

Most promoters would at least make a modicum of effort to meet their contractual obligations, but it was not to be, this time. This tour was not any of that. Grand pianos that were not grand, or in tune; sound systems that couldn't produce tolerable quality sound; stages that were the size of small dining rooms; dressing rooms like coat closets – all of it was bad, bad, bad.

Late one night, I was sitting in my London hotel room writing a letter of encouragement to a female friend who was being frequently knocked around by her boyfriend. Suddenly, the Lord began speaking into my head. I knew it was Him. It was almost like a tape recording – very factual and straightforward. He said I would return to Point Dume (north of Malibu) after the tour, and sometime soon afterwards I would see a newspaper headline reporting a nuclear accident at San Onofre Nuclear Power Plant (later known as SONGS). From that moment I would have two weeks to tidy up my affairs and I would leave California. Then, the meeting was over. No Q&A time, no follow-up. I was puzzled. I had heard from the Lord, and I had had these premonition-type "knowings" before, but not anything like this. This was a whole new level and it really got my attention.

I flew back into the U.S. through New York City, and I called Al Staehely to see if he could pick me up from the airport when I arrived at LAX. He kindly agreed and I gave him my flight number. On our ride back up the Pacific Coast Highway out of Santa Monica, I related to him the disaster of the road trip and also told him about the "vision." We agreed to meet for breakfast the next morning and do some additional catching-up. I asked him not to come too early as I really needed a good night's sleep. That was probably around midnight. At around seven o'clock the next morning there was a knock at my door. I looked over at the clock and couldn't believe it – WAY too early. I went to the front door and there stood Al, with a newspaper up in front of his face:

The headline read:

"Southland A-Plant Damaged in Nuclear Accident"
Dateline: San Onofre

Surprise doesn't even begin to describe it. I felt numb and a bit distressed, but also very curious. I had assumed that the Lord was talking weeks or months, not the day after I got back. This had a very short fuse. I quickly dressed and we went down to the Point Dume Café, which was at the bottom of the hill from where I lived. After we looked over the menus and ordered, he quietly asked, "Well, what are you going to do?" Without any hesitation I responded, "I'm leaving California within two weeks." The only things I didn't know were – to where, and, what would I do when I got there? I had done a lot of thinking as I had traveled about the country regarding where I might want to live, someday. Two places came to mind: Richmond, Virginia and Austin, Texas. I had really enjoyed Richmond and felt very much at home, there. I also knew I would not go back to Corpus Christi, which still seemed lost in a time warp. But this had to happen, right away. Getting connected to Richmond would take time. I enjoyed Austin and the surrounding hill country and I had some family in that area, so I decided to head to Austin. I met with the guys in Jo Jo Gunne and told them what had transpired. I enjoyed their camaraderie and enjoyed traveling with them, but this was happening. They really didn't have much to say other than "good luck and stay in touch." I don't think they had ever experienced anything like this. Neither had I. I sold some things, gave away some things, packed my fairly new VW bus with what was left and headed for Texas.

The Alpha Male

Back in Austin I enrolled back into UT in the School of Radio, Television and Film and applied for a job doing maintenance and studio cleanup at Odyssey Sound Studios on 6th Street. I spoke with the principal owner, Jay Aaron Podolnick, and made my pitch for a grunge position, doing maintenance, troubleshooting, and sweeping the floors. He thought that was ridiculous and told me that I had more practical experience than any of the guys currently running the place, and I should become his first-call engineer.

It was an immediate delight for me – I suddenly had an entire 24 track studio at my fingertips – the only one in Central Texas – and plenty of time to learn more about this enchanted little getaway from the outside world. My UT professors were grateful for the opportunity to come see a real studio – an unsettling fact when I realized that I knew more about studios and the record business than they did. Jay treated me exceptionally well and I was back in school at UT, and cutting records and demos. My personal life still lay in a freezer box, somewhere in a dark storeroom. My social skills and my ability to negotiate and navigate in relationships were all based on business activities – not personal matters.

The business grew slowly, with periods of white knuckle survival in that dusty little town in Central Texas. One day Michael Brovsky showed up from New York City with Free Flow Productions, along with Jerry Jeff Walker and the Lost Gonzo Band. I became Michael's first-call engineer and I considered Redneck Cowboy to be the taxes I paid in order to do what I really liked – blues, rock, blues-rock, and jazz-rock. Probably one of my favorite album projects of all time was the ElectroMagnets, featuring Eric Johnson on guitar. I really enjoyed working with so many of the highly talented local musicians who needed demo tapes in order to get jobs.

John H. Ingle

I talked Jay and his partner Steve Shields into letting me and my sidekick, the late Larson Lundahl, open a 4-track demo studio next door in what had been our very large storeroom. We called it Last Minute Productions. We would cut demos there and masters in the big studio. Our plan was to train all that local talent in how to get their music to come across in the studio. The talent was plentiful but their level of studio experience was not. Their success would become our success. Our business card logo was a rabbit holding a pocket watch, à la Alice in Wonderland.

Many of our customers were people I'd known somewhat from before Los Angeles, such as Stevie Vaughn and his brother Jimmie along with their crews. Their sessions were paid for by a kindly mother hen and mentor, Shirley Dimmick, who also would bring in Denny Freeman and other blues players. I would later discover that she was Shirley Ratisseau, an iconic blues legend from an era gone by. She was the first well-known white female blues singer to front a "mixed-race band." Shirley was quiet and supportive, but she could crack the whip, as well. One night Stevie's band had decided that it was time for Stevie to quit hiding behind his guitar and to get up to the microphone and do a lead vocal. We laid down the basic track and prepared for the vocal. Lars shuttled the tape back and forth to record the track without Stevie singing a single note. Each time during tape rewind I was reassuring and calm, softly urging into the talkback mike, "That's okay, you'll get it. Let's go one more time." Each time he would lean into the microphone like a ten year old boy hugging home plate at bat for the first time. But, then he would jump back from the imaginary fastball at the last second as the starting point of his vocal flew by on the tape. At about the seventh pass with no joy, I looked at Shirley and she looked at me. I wasn't used to dealing with singers who didn't want to sing. I asked her if she could offer Stevie some help. Shirley's son

The Alpha Male

Laine began talking to her – something like, "Remember in Beaumont when the Big Bopper would come out to the ball park and visit and he brought Janis (Joplin) out to meet you? If you were able to teach Janis to sing, you can teach Stevie." I looked back to Shirley. "Really? You taught Janis to sing?" "Well, I did work with her some at the park," Shirley allowed. She came forward and pressed the talkback button: "Stevie, if I say you can sing, you can SING! Now, sing, dammit!" We ran the tape again and Stevie stayed in the batter's box at home plate and sailed nonstop through the track, putting down a very respectable vocal track. When he came back into the control room, the band sort of jostled around with shocked goofy grins on their faces, bumping shoulders with him, and giggling. You could hear them thinking, "Dang...Stevie can sing!" I remember thinking, "Hmm, that's interesting...Stevie, can sing." A couple of years later, the record company's marketing department would add his middle name, Ray, to his new band's name. To us, he was still just Stevie, but he could sing. And, he could play a guitar.

A few weeks later, Lars and I were setting up for a small country-folk band demo, when in walked a beautiful brunette carrying her guitar case. She walked into the studio main room, set her case down, and with a big smile, looked back into the control room towards us through the triple glass window. I smiled back at her, turned to Lars and saw that he was already well aware of her presence. I told Lars, "I'm going to marry that girl." He looked at me, chuckling almost sheepishly, and said something approximating, "Yeah, right."

Sure enough, I married that girl. God told me not to do it. I told Him, "It's okay. I've got this." The night I told Him that, as I tried to sleep, I felt a wave of anxiety roll over me and tears seeped into my pillow. I knew at that moment that I had crossed a line somewhere that I could not even identify or describe at that moment. But, I thought sure it could work out. It wasn't long before I realized that our marriage was truly exciting – exciting as in a flaming torch glued to one hand and a bucket of gasoline glued to the other. Her Post-Traumatic Stress Disorder was worse than mine. I was outside the camp, again, in a big way. I thought I could save her. She would prove to me that I could not.

The music business grew and prospered and our surrounding tribe of studio musicians became more sophisticated and professional. For a studio backup band I had Chris Geppert, and his band, Flash, who would soon become known as Christopher Cross. For first call piano I had Reese Wynans, who would go on to play keyboards for Stevie Ray Vaughan and other great bands. For guitars, I had John Staehely as well as Eric Johnson, who would be featured multiple times on the front cover of Guitar Player™ magazine. Life was mostly good, at least on the business front. Success was starting to warm up behind the curtains, stage-left. But, along with success came all the trappings – drugs, alcohol and egos – egos the size of small continents. With money coming in, the type of drugs and hangers-on around the studio changed. I began to see a lot more cocaine – The Big Liar. I had already learned about cocaine in LA. Cocaine will tell you that those tracks you just recorded were fantastic – full of energy and brilliance. The next day they would prove to be neither. The Big Liar knows how to waste money, time and people. I'm sure the devil loves cocaine. I started a low-key campaign against it in my sessions. Over time I became more vocal and then lost a major client because of my outspoken position. At the same time I found myself in business situations that I didn't like. I was into a whole new kind of bad behavior and I didn't like it.

Not long after that we had a son and the Lord suddenly took me out of the music business as my regular profession. He told me to tell my

The Alpha Male

business partners that I didn't want anything from them – it was all theirs – He would provide what I needed. I still worked with Malcolm Harper's Reelsound Recording on an occasional live concert recording for several more years, but I had walked away from all of what I had invested business-wise and my career in show business was ended. The Lord sent me back, one time, to warn my former business partners of their impending huge success and that it would be dangerous for them all. I didn't know if they could hear me. The huge success came and so did the huge danger, but I was not there to live through it with them. But, I missed it all, terribly – not the business, but the music, the excitement and many of the people that I had grown up with in the business.

I moved my family well out into the hill country – away from show business and the people who ran it, and were run by it. My wife's PTSD was no better in our rural isolation. Divorce came to my house and tore it up. Seven years of highly emotional roller-coaster survival was over. I moved east of Austin into old farm country, with my four year old son Joshua, and continued to work for a Texas oil and ranch family as their estate manager. Josh and I attended a *really* small Baptist Church near Webberville. Everyone literally knew everyone, and probably half the church was related to each other. I was listening for God's voice and I had a contentment with my life that was only overshadowed by not having a woman – a wife – to share it with. I was back in the land of potato salad and fried chicken, but I was hoping and praying for a break in my spiritual life that would reveal a bigger plan for me. Then, one Sunday morning in the fall of 1984 a new girl showed up at church. Hmm. Interesting…and cute. But, I knew I still wasn't ready for a new relationship.

After the morning service I approached this young lady stranger about getting together to play cards – it could get really too quiet out in the country, sometimes. She agreed and was looking for the same thing. We started out "just friends" and played cards and sat and sipped hot tea and talked on cold winter nights. We enjoyed each other's company and the time we spent together. She and Josh got along great. One day I came by her workplace to "talk." I met her out in the parking lot. I told her I loved her. I had realized that I wanted her with me, from now on. She cried. Much later, she said that when I told her I loved her, she suddenly could see her whole future spread out before her – kids, the whole thing. I asked her to marry me. "Maybe," she said. I gave her some time and then I asked again. "Most probably," she hedged. I told her I was going to bust. I had to know, one way or the other. She told me later that she had made some bad decisions about men in her life and felt as if she couldn't really trust her feelings. She talked to her dad about me. "He's not like any of the other men I've ever dated." "Well, thank God," her daddy replied. She told her mom that I had asked her to marry and she wanted to know whether she should or not. Mom said, "Yes." That was good enough for me, so, it was settled. Thanks, mom.

Marriage is not easy, even when both parties are trying the best that they're able. I lost Josh in a gut-wrenching custody battle. I had been laid off from my job when oil sank to $11 per barrel. The economy went into a death spiral in Texas, and took many of the banks with it. It was known as the Savings and Loan disaster, but it spilled over into everything else. There were no jobs – of ANY kind. Every job advertisement was met with a two-block-long line of applicants, and potential employers wanted a college diploma for a job sweeping the warehouse. Shortly after the layoff I was in a bad auto accident and had some injuries and surgeries that slowed me down and made me even more unemployable for a while. Not only did I not yet have a degree, but I couldn't stack boxes in a warehouse, either. I started to suffer from bouts of severe depression. It was getting very hard to provide for my family. Times were desperate and getting worse. I began to get angry with God for leaving me feeling as if I were roasting over a slow burning fire. Over the next couple of years, I began to pull back into the shell that I had just recently managed to crawl out of. I stopped listening.

Most of us can reasonably assume that we can put the next meal on the table, somehow. Most anyone of us can develop marketable skills if we work at it. But, after significant trauma in our lives, many of us may not be able to feel safe – safe from physical or emotional attack, safe from predatory actions that take away our home or our job, or our only source of food or water. A traumatic event in our lives can make us feel continually threatened that we won't be able to be physically safe and have our essential needs met. A series of multiple traumatic events can make recovery and a future seem impossible.

Traumatic events abound in this world; a horrific travel accident; parents that deal drugs and allow violent and predatory people near their children; door-to-door combat; childhood sexual abuse. The list of traumatic events that can befall a child is substantial, and very real. Shocking statistics on how many children suffer sexual abuse make one shake their head and ask, "Who are these people that do this to children?" Those battered, mangled, and bruised children grow up. They will attempt to satisfy those elementary human urges that we all share – the basic needs of water, food, sleep, and sex – a job, friends, families of their own. The fact that they are badly broken doesn't eradicate those basic human drives – they are going to try to find those essential elements and make them part of their lives. In the meanwhile, people crave safety, especially these battered and bruised former children.

In the history of psychology and sociology, you can see the evidence that safety and peace are a basic necessity of civilization and order. If you've studied in the areas of sociology and psychology, you are bound to have come across Maslow and his pyramid of the hierarchy (pecking order) of human needs.

Maslow and the Hierarchy of Needs - The Pyramid

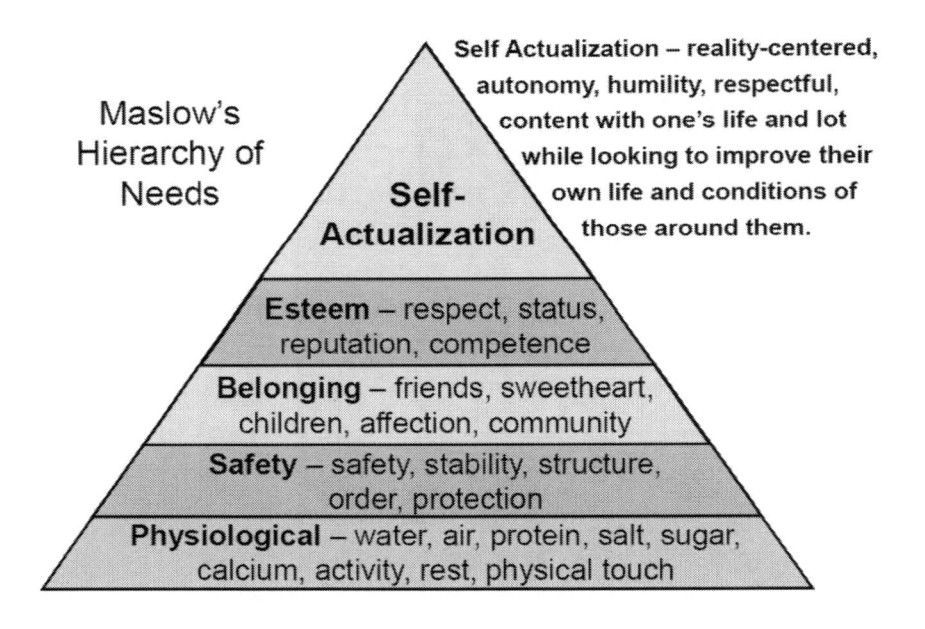

Maslow's Hierarchy of Needs

- **Self-Actualization** – reality-centered, autonomy, humility, respectful, content with one's life and lot while looking to improve their own life and conditions of those around them.
- **Esteem** – respect, status, reputation, competence
- **Belonging** – friends, sweetheart, children, affection, community
- **Safety** – safety, stability, structure, order, protection
- **Physiological** – water, air, protein, salt, sugar, calcium, activity, rest, physical touch

Maslow's pyramid begins at the bottom with physical survival and keeps going up in steps to the very top step which he called "Self-Actualization" – who am I, and why? What is my purpose? What grand mark can I leave on the world to let them know that I once lived? What can I do for others? Mankind's traditional view of the world uses this "bottom > up" perspective when looking at life and survival. We concentrate on meeting our basic needs and then, eventually, we look up to see what's going on around us, and what we can do for others.

The Alpha Male

The Lord has a different perspective that He would prefer that you use. Instead of you carrying the pyramid around on your shoulders, He inverts the pyramid and invites you to step out onto the top and begins to give you answers to all your questions about – "Who are you?" "What is your purpose?" "What can you do for others?" Then, way down at the bottom of the list He says:

> *"So do not worry, saying, 'What shall we eat?' or 'What shall we drink?' or 'What shall we wear?' For the pagans run after all these things, and your heavenly Father knows that you need them. But seek first his kingdom and his righteousness, and all these things will be given to you as well" (Matthew 6:31-33).*

His Kingdom is about being sons and daughters of The Most High – princes and princesses. This is really important and we'll take this urgent matter up again, shortly.

Chapter 6 – Not the Alpha Male? (Build the Man)

What if you suddenly discover, as I did, that you are *not* the Alpha Male? Don't freak out. It can happen and has probably happened at some point in life to the vast majority of men, whether they admit to it or not. But, here's the good part. You may have lost a little time getting there, but don't fret over the unchangeable past. Look towards the changeable future. The real objective is to arrive where God wants you, and if you're alive enough to read this, there is still time. The Lord God of the Universe is waiting for you to crash into that reality so that He can get your attention and talk to you.

There is No Auto-pilot

I've done a lot of flying in my lifetime, usually either commercial or military, typically as a passenger but sometimes in the right hand seat, and sometimes in the "jump seat." I think my first flight was with my dad in a Cessna 140A, at about the age of 12. He taught flight instrumentation classes for pilots wanting to elevate their license from Visual Flight Rules to Instrument Flight Rules. Due to his instructor status he was allowed to maintain his hours using the school's available aircraft. That ride in the Cessna was my first time to take the yoke and point an airplane somewhere. So, I like flying metaphors. In life, first of all, you must remember that there is no: autopilot; Automatic Direction Finder; Instrument Landing System; or Auto-Land. None of these are available for you to depend on. Well, okay, they *are* there, but you absolutely do *not* want to use them. Because if you do, it's a guarantee that the evil of this world will be in there feeding phony course headings into it, and SHAZZAM! You're lost, off-course and don't even know how you got there, and, oops, there's a mountain in front of you as you come out of that cloud and you're at the wrong altitude and on the wrong heading.

Living is all done in *manual mode* – forget auto-pilot, or auto-anything – it's *hands-on*. If you find yourself fat, dumb, and contented and it's all Happy Trails and Easter Eggs, then you probably are on auto-pilot and you need to grab the joystick or yoke quickly, before you come out of the clouds and find yourself staring at the side of a very large mountain!

Gaining Control

Control of your life belongs to you. It doesn't belong to the modern culture, your friends at work, your employer, or your classmates. God made you to be free. Your decisions and the moves you make in life belong to you. You will find yourself needing a lot of wise counsel, but the moves are your own. No one makes them for you unless you abandon the authority to be in control of your life. The Lord God that created you is the best wise counsel there is, anywhere. So, are you listening to that counsel? Your first challenge will be to admit that you are not God – you don't know everything, and you're not the most awesome thing to ever hit the universe. After you discover that He is your best counsel, how do you go about hearing Him? It's not like you can just ring Him up on the phone, right? Or, maybe you can. God is speaking into your life. Wouldn't you like to know what He's saying? Of course you would.

Hearing God's Voice

In approximately the spring of 2003, I had purchased my first boat in many years. It was a 20' Nitro Bass & Ski outboard, a type of boat I'd never owned before. It was sleek and fast, with a 175hp outboard motor and held six people easily. The man I bought it from said it would do 70mph flat out on smooth water. We were putting it into the water for the first time since we had purchased it a month or so earlier, and as it rolled slowly off the trailer into the water I began to crank the engine. We moved slowly out of the cove towards the main part of the lake.

As we were cruising along I tried to mess with the motor trim and I pushed the throttle forward all the way and brought the motor higher out of the water. The bow rose up and we seemed to just stall where we were. I slowed down and tried it again. I went to the rear of the boat to the large stowage area where all the batteries are and the pumps and so forth, in front of the motor. When I lifted the lid I was shocked to see water steadily filling the whole compartment. I panicked. I turned on the bilge pump but that didn't seem to be doing much to help the situation, even though a steady stream of water, larger than my thumb, was pumping out the side of the boat. I immediately turned the boat around and headed for the boat ramp area. I passed my father-in-law, Paw-Paw Herman, in his pontoon boat, and yelled out that we were taking on water – a lot of it. He followed us back and I asked him what to do. I semi-beached the boat but the 20' foot long boat was still a long way out into the water and the batteries were about to go underwater. There was no time to go get the truck and trailer. Paw-Paw said that he didn't know anything about that kind of boat, and he

The Alpha Male

took off around the corner of the cove to see if his son, Bill, was around at his lake house.

Paw-Paw blasted up to Bill's dock where Bill was fishing off the end of it. He stopped the boat right beside him and said, "Bill, get in the boat!" Bill dropped his fishing rod, jumped into the boat and they took off back to the beach area where we were all frantically bailing out the bilge with plastic drinking cups. The first thing Bill asked was, "Did you put in the bilge plugs?" Ummm… Uhhh… Whut? Oh….yeah. The bilge plugs, those little rubbery mechanical stoppers that plug up the drain holes in the bottom of the boat. That's why we were sinking – there were holes in the bottom of the boat…holes that I was supposed to put plugs into in order to keep the boat from sinking…duh.

But the part that stuck with me the most all these years was not so much the lesson of the plugs for the bilge drains, but the fact that when Paw-Paw said, "Bill, get in the boat," Bill just dropped his fishing rod right there on the dock, and jumped into the boat, without any hesitation, or a single question. I was amazed. I thought of my own possible reaction to that surprising request, had the roles been reversed. I might have told Paw-Paw that I have to put away my tackle, or change my shoes, or run tell my wife, or wash my car, and then I could go as soon as that was done. Then, I wondered…how many times has the Lord told me, "John, get in the boat"? And, there I stood, with a list of twenty questions, or things I would do first, check them off, one by one, and then I would get into the boat…if it were still there.

In the fall of 2006 the Lord gave me a vision to underscore what he was telling me about hearing his voice. He gave me a mental picture of a very diligent servant with MP3 player headphones on, running the vacuum cleaner, carefully cleaning those living room carpets. The

47

doorbell began to ring. From another room the Master of the House was calling. The servant doesn't hear him because of the noise, the music in his headphones, and the servant's intense focus on what he's doing. The servant doesn't hear the master calling, "Answer the door!" And, there at the door was an opportunity that the Lord was inviting the servant to enjoy. He had already prepared it, and it was a lovely opportunity. He wanted that servant to have it...but the servant couldn't hear the Master saying, "John, answer the door."

In late January of 2007, the Lord gave me another vision. I had been praying earnestly for many years for more understanding of how I was supposed to relate to what God was doing, and had been doing, and would keep doing, for time immemorial. Where did I fit in? He showed me a scene from the Old Testament (He doesn't call it that) wherein Joshua was leading the children of Israel against armies of invaders. And, "the Lord cast great stones down from Heaven" (Joshua 10:11 KJV) upon the armies of the enemy and more were killed by the stones than by the battle with the Israelites.

Now, I had wondered about that passage many times, even as a boy. I was perplexed how the Lord could/would do such a thing. After all, there are physics at work here. Where in the world did these stones come from that He hurled down upon the enemy? (I know that some translations interpret this passage to be talking about ice hailstones, but this is what I heard from the Lord.) How did they only strike down the armies of their enemies? Did the Lord suddenly call the stones into creation, and then put them into a trajectory to land on that plain, 10 years later, smacking only the enemy? The Lord told me "The stones were already coming..."

What he wanted to show me was that Joshua wasn't responsible for the stones' arrival, but because Joshua was open and listening to the

Lord, the Lord was able to show Joshua where the Israelites needed to stand, so that they wouldn't be wiped out by the stones. *That* is what is so important. The Lord has set many things in motion in both the physical and spiritual world. The stones were already coming – maybe for a million years – and then they arrived. Maybe more stones are coming. There are, most assuredly, *many more* stones coming. Wouldn't it be nice if we would be listening when He says, "Move over there, on that other hill?" Or, maybe, "Sell that stock, or that property, or buy this other property." Or, even, "Take your child out of public school for this next year." Or, "Show your wife more affection." Or, "Your son-in-law needs you to love him even though he's not perfect."

If all these things are already set in motion (ever read the books of Daniel, or Revelation?) then we surely need guidance from the only source that knows where to be and what to be doing when those "stones" arrive. Who else is able to do such a thing? Us? Surely, not. God's word makes it clear how sharp and dependable we are on our own, and with such perfect wisdom and vision. Hmm…maybe not…so, we need to make sure that we're listening so that we know where to stand, because, for sure, more stones are coming.

Use Your Faith

"Use your faith." That's what the Lord said to me at 3:30 a.m. I was sleeping soundly, but I was having a disturbing dream wherein my wife and I were meeting with a client and he became distraught over some news we had given him and then he announced that we were no longer going to do business together. Our business relationship had been rocky recently due to reasons which weren't very clear. As in all matters that happen in the earthly realm, there is opportunity for things to work out in a way you had not planned or wanted. I awoke from the dream and began to ask the Lord what was going on in our business that things were so rough lately and people were so agitated and nervous. And, why were our business relationships suddenly so strained?

As I lay there on my pillow looking up into the night, He said, "Use your faith." Wow, what an answer! That means that as far as the Lord was concerned, I had *not* been using my faith. What a wakeup call! I was not using my faith! And, of course, He hit the nail right on the head, just like He always does. No, I wasn't using my faith. I wasn't speaking in faith, I wasn't acting in faith, and I wasn't living in faith. I was living in a world of men (and women) and I was trying to please them. I wasn't trying to please God, and I wasn't working for God. I guess I had changed jobs without even realizing it. I was completely wrapped up in the world of men and their expectations, their faults, their mistakes, their laziness, their lack of accountability, their and my inability to walk the perfect life.

Oh, great, I was back in the world, working in a job where there was absolutely no chance of success, or happiness, or peace, or love. I was standing in the wrong place and the stones were falling all around me, and *on* me – and, they HURT. I prayed for about an hour, asking God to forgive me for my stubbornness, and for me ignoring Him in my life, except to complain to Him when things weren't going like I planned. I finished my prayer by asking the Lord to confirm this to me in my morning Bible time.

When I awoke the next morning, very bleary-eyed, I rambled downstairs, poured some coffee and turned on the morning news. Occasionally, I would tune in to Dr. Ira Hilliard, a pastor with an early morning television show. Instead of the newscast I expected to see, there he was, walking back and forth at the edge of the stage, holding

The Alpha Male

his Bible out in his hand. He was recalling how when he started his current ministry that He felt God calling him to "teach the Bible." All his advisors and associates warned him, "No, no. That isn't going to work." And he did it anyway, because that's what he saw God calling him to do. He said that he had to quit living to please men. He had to follow, and needed to live, God's plan. Then the dream-state returned. It was as if I was back on my pillow staring at the ceiling in the dark. "Quit living for men – you aren't going to please them and you'll waste your time and your energy trying. And you won't be standing in the right place at the right time." Wow, there it was! That was my confirmation with a few more hints as to why things were going so badly. My life was filled with anxiety and frustration. I was being pelted by all those stones that were landing on me. I was standing in the wrong place! I wasn't standing under God's covering. I wasn't doing God's plan. I was running around trying to please men and find "success"!! But, here I was, standing in the wrong place, and these stones were beginning to hurt, and they were falling all around me. They were hitting me and my wife and my children and it wasn't stopping. How is it that I keep doing that? Well, according to God, it was because I wasn't listening. I wasn't HEARING His voice. Hmm...that means if I'm not listening then I don't know where to be standing, and what to be doing there.

So, it's obvious that if I'm supposed to be listening, then my most important job is being ready and able to hear God speak. I need to hear God's voice in my life. So, **Job One** is to hear God's voice. If I can't do that, I can't proceed with anything but my own ideas. That's not a good plan and I have the proof in the bumps, bruises, and scars all over me and my family from these stones.

Look at that statement, "Use your faith." Surely, we all know about faith. You're supposed to *have faith*. Just "have" it. But God didn't say to me, "Have faith." He said, "Use your faith." That moved it from passive to active. I actually had to do something with it. If I "...have faith as a grain of mustard seed," Jesus said, "you would say..." He didn't say, "This would happen," or "That would happen," Jesus said, "You would say..." That's not passive, folks, that's active. That's not observer status – that's a participant! So, I "will *say*, to this mountain, 'Move from here to there,' and it will move. There is nothing that would be impossible to you." That's a great big difference from the stones, and the cuts, bruises, and the chaos that runs rampant, otherwise. That is some kind of awesome power. But it's not a power that has no context. Using that power obviously requires that it is used in a manner in which God intended. What did He intend? Well, that's the part where we have to hear His voice.

Life goes on and on. It seems sometimes as we look back through history that there is no end. But, as believers, we know that is a function of our short physical lives on this plane. Napoleon seems like an eternity ago, although blood ran through his veins in the same manner as it runs through yours and mine. The pyramids of Egypt are unfathomable in time. Heck, my teenage years are starting to fade into The Middle Ages, or at least the Revolutionary War. So, is famine coming? Are political instability and civil unrest coming? We can all sit around and get agitated about what might happen in the earthly realm. Who's to know? Well, God knows. He's speaking quietly to you right now if you listen. And, then, when you listen and *hear*, then you are ready to "Use your faith." Big Red Flag - worrying interferes with hearing God's voice. Jesus advised us to consider whether by worrying we could make ourselves taller.

When we don't use our faith, and end up not standing in the right place, we get beat up by the stones. And then we're tempted to whine and say, "Oh, Boo-Hoo, Jesus doesn't care about me, anymore. He always

The Alpha Male

liked Charlie, or Alice, or Betsy (somebody else) better. He blesses them even when they don't deserve it any more than I do." Nonsense! Jesus hasn't brought either you or me this far so that we can fall flat on our face and be made a laughingstock. He wants us to be an effective witness for the power of God. He wants us to "finish the race." We can get there in a number of ways. He can save us at the very last moment and demonstrate how He can bail us out at the doorstep of Hell's front gate! *That's* a witness. Or, He could help us in our daily walk with Him so that we are a light to the darkness…salt for the flavor…living waters that flow from Him, through us, to a dry and dusty world that is parched with thirst. I'm pretty sure He wants that one, and not the first one.

I've sometimes wondered if I could go back to the music world that I left and be a witness for Christ. I've often wondered why the Lord pulled me out of that so that it seemed that there was no way I could return. I must admit, I love music. I didn't care much for the business, but I love music. I love to help build it, arrange it, and record it in a studio environment. Maybe that's why He took me away from it – it was too much of a temptation for me to love the music more than Him. If that's the case, then I thank Him for that, because it, no doubt, would be interfering with me hearing His voice. Thinking about going back to the music world as a witness brought me to think about a certain friend. My friend's life had fallen completely apart. Our relationship had been rocky over the years, and we had sometimes been at odds with each other over serious issues. Since he fell into grim and wanton sin, his life had disintegrated, and I had wondered if the Lord would have me reach out to him and witness to him, even though it seemed clear he didn't want to hear from me about anything. He had claimed to be saved in the past, but only he and the Lord know that one. But, the Lord gave me a vision – he showed me a prison cell. In that cell, the prisoners were huddled and hunkered down. They paid very little attention to each other. But, each time someone on the outside of the cell approached, they all immediately stood up and stepped forward, wanting to see if that person was there to see them and what that person might be bringing them. Then, it struck me. The prisoners saw their fellow prisoners around them as no better off than themselves. Their fellow prisoners were practically invisible. They presumed that their fellow prisoners had nothing to offer; no safety, no freedom, and nothing worth hearing. They expected that someone on the outside of the cell *did* have something to offer, and wanted to hear it, or receive it. It seemed that the Lord was telling me that this individual, whose life was in shambles, had been too close in my life for too long, and that, in his eyes, I was just another fellow prisoner, regardless of who I really am. I had no witness with him. So, I began to pray that the Lord would send a witness to him that he could see and hear – someone whose presence there would be noticed, and their word heard. I think there is great truth here and I'm not sure that I fully understand it. It may be closely related to what Jesus said about doing miracles in his own town. He also said that there were many lepers in Elijah's town, but only the foreigner came to be healed. The lepers may all have thought that Elijah was in the same cell with them.

However, there are also times when the Lord *does* want to send you – maybe someplace you don't really want to go. You might find yourself saying, in similar fashion to Jonah, "Alright, alright, I'll go to Nineveh. But, if I go, I'm going to want to see some fire and brimstone! I want to see some Sodom and Gomorrah action, and some sand melting into glass!" Can I get an "Amen"? Okay, no, let's not get an amen on that one. Because the moment you want to see punishment, or payback, you've put on the robes of the Judge and clawed your way up to the Master's bench to hand out punishment to the evildoers. Is that your job? No. Jesus said not to judge or YOU will be judged. Pretty firm warning, that one. So, what *you* want to see is the Mercy Seat, the source of God's love for *you*. You are His favorite part of Creation. It is *your* redemption, there on the Mercy Seat that He's talking about.

> *"And there I will meet with thee, and I will commune with thee from above the mercy seat, from between the two cherubim which are upon the ark of the testimony..." (Exodus 25:22 KJV).*

The blood sprinkled on the Mercy Seat covered the sins of the people. God was foretelling the shedding of Jesus' blood on our behalf as the final and permanent, perfect sacrifice – the one that would restore man to his designed relationship with the Father. Jesus' blood becomes the ultimate solution to the demands of the Law and its requirement for blood in order to forgive sin. When we want punishment for the offenders we become the judge, where our flesh *often* wants to take us. Paul said that "I war daily." I fully expect this is one of the things against which he would have had to war, just as we do.

More recently in my life, one night between Thanksgiving and Christmas, I was asleep, dreaming and the Lord interrupted my dream to tell me that a Christian brother's business was going through some very difficult times. I had not been aware of it. He told me that I was to call my brother and tell him that in the coming February his business would completely turn around and begin to prosper, greatly. I awoke and pondered what the Lord had just told me. I thought to myself that it was practically the middle of the night and I would wait and call during the next day. I went back to sleep and slept soundly for a bit – perhaps a couple of hours. The Lord interrupted another dream and spoke again, but this time He asked, "Well, are you going to tell him, or not?" I immediately awoke and looked at the clock. It was about 5:30 in the morning. Well, I need to get up and make a phone call. I kicked off the coffee maker a little earlier than usual and went for my phone. I called the brother and told him what the Lord had told me. He thanked me for calling and for being faithful to relay what I had heard. I checked back with him several months later, and true to His word, in February the embattled business suddenly turned around and began to prosper, greatly. Sometimes, God has words for us that aren't for us. He calls that "prophecy." He uses us for the delivery of those words for various reasons that we don't necessarily understand. In the world of Biblical times, to prophesy means to speak on behalf of God. In this case, I think it was a witness to what He was about to do in that brother's life, so that there was no mistake as to what was about to happen and who had brought it about.

Faith is a Catalyst

Think back to chemistry class where you probably heard about and studied catalysts. A catalyst is defined as a substance that *causes* or *accelerates* a chemical reaction without being consumed by it. You can recover it and use it, again. Your faithfulness – your faithful action – is an activator, or catalyst. It is an energy source that brings authority or power to a situation and pours into it. The result is that something happens that you might not have otherwise seen happen, or it happens much faster than you would have expected.

The Parable of the Persistent Widow

Jesus told his disciples a parable to demonstrate persistence in their prayers. The parable was of a woman desiring justice who kept coming to a judge with her plea. The judge didn't fear God and had no compassion for man or his problems. But, he finally decided to see to it that the woman received her justice because he saw that she wasn't going to quit.

The Alpha Male

> *"'Though I have no fear of God and no respect for anyone, yet because this widow keeps bothering me, I will grant her justice, so that she may not wear me out by continually coming.' And the Lord said, 'Listen to what the unjust judge says. And will not God grant justice to his chosen ones who cry to him day and night?'" (Luke 18:4-7a, NRSV).*

Jesus appears to be giving them a lesson in both faith and persistence. Faith and persistence combined become *faithfulness*. On another occasion Jesus was brought a boy that the disciples had been unable to heal from his demon possession. Jesus rebuked the demon and healed the boy. The disciples were puzzled at not being able to drive the demon out, and were looking for an explanation. They considered that they had done everything just as Jesus had taught them. Jesus replied,

> "Because you have so little faith. I tell you the truth, if you have faith as small as a mustard seed, you can say to this mountain, 'Move from here to there' and it will move. Nothing will be impossible for you" (Matthew 17:20).

It surely does look like Jesus was explaining the virtues of both faith and persistence, in combination. He was encouraging them, and us, to use both. Don't stop just because you don't see immediate results.

Knowledge and Wisdom

There's an old saying, "When all you have is a hammer, everything looks like a nail." It's not a particularly elegant saying, but very useful to contemplate. When our skills and knowledge are limited, we tend to see through a dark and narrow corridor to the problems that arise, and the decisions that need to be made to deal with them. Acquiring additional skills and knowledge allows us to enlarge that view, and to have a bigger toolbox from which to select, instead of being limited to pounding everything with a hammer, when what you needed was a screwdriver. I believe that the Lord is always trying to widen our vision, so that we can make room for what He wants to do, instead of approaching everything with a hammer.

There's another old saying, "Knowledge is – knowing that a tomato is a fruit. Wisdom is – knowing not to put it in the fruit salad."

> *"Get wisdom, get understanding; do not forget my words or turn away from them. Do not forsake wisdom, and she will protect you; love her, and she will watch over you. The beginning of wisdom is this: Get wisdom"* (Proverbs 4:5-7).

So, <u>Get</u> Wisdom. It's the beginning.

Very early in the beginning of wisdom it's helpful to understand certain, basic ground rules.

1. It all belongs to God.
2. He loves you, mightily.
3. He wants to share it with you.
4. Jesus has the guest list, and the backstage passes.
5. You're invited – but you have to RSVP – that is, accept the invitation, and then follow His directions on how to get to the celebration.

Wisdom is like a set of filters that allows us to block the earthly distractions and chaos of daily life so that we aren't constantly being drug off the path into the weeds. Wisdom is a perimeter defense that gives us time to consider what's going on and to hear the Spirit speak into our lives. Maturity is the continuous application of wisdom to the circumstances of life. It is not like being pregnant – a binary yes or no descriptor – it is a continuum, a sliding scale, so that as we apply more and more wisdom to our lives, maturity is what the people around us begin to notice – something has changed. In every situation in which you live, the Lord sets opportunities before you to gain both knowledge and wisdom. I believe that He does this so that we are able to humble ourselves in that situation, knowing that He is still Lord God Almighty, and we're not.

As we walk through life, we sometimes find ourselves looking for happiness and satisfaction (joy) upon our arrival at some future destination, to which we've not yet arrived. Our not-having-arrived-yet leaves us in a state of limbo, unable to enjoy where we are. We become dependent upon the success of that someday future situation that we fantasize is going to "put us there," in a state of triumph over the obstacles that stand in our way. This is not likely to happen. Failing to seek God in every situation, putting off joy and peace, leaves us longing for something that never arrives. The goalposts keep moving as we get closer, always striving, but never arriving. No peace. No joy. No knowledge. No wisdom.

> *"But if people are bound in chains, held fast by cords of affliction, He tells them what they have done—that they have sinned arrogantly. He makes them listen to correction and commands them to repent of their evil. If they obey and serve Him, they will spend the rest of their days in prosperity and their years in contentment. But if they do not listen, they will perish by the sword and die without knowledge" (Job 36:8-12).*

Being held fast by the cords of affliction, which is our egotistical sin – that we think we know what should really be happening. Why doesn't God get with the program? Well, God's program is YOU.

> *"He is wooing you from the jaws of distress to a spacious place free from restriction, to the comfort of your table laden with choice food," (Job 36:16).*
>
> *"Remember to extol his work, which people have praised in song. All humanity has seen it; mortals gaze on it from afar. How great is God—beyond our understanding! The number of his years is past finding out" (Job 36:24-26).*

So, really our focus should be on extolling (praising) His work; rejoicing in who He is, and that He is our Creator and Provider. He is our Daddy – Abba Father. If we're doing that, suddenly our dissatisfaction and our arrogance fade away and are replaced by joy and contentment, and we find ourselves living in that "spacious place free from restriction."

> *"The Almighty is beyond our reach and exalted in power; in His justice and great righteousness, He does not oppress. Therefore, people revere Him, for does He not have regard for all the wise in heart?" (Job 37:23-24).*

So, if you're being oppressed, it's probably *you* doing the oppressing, operating in pride and in dissatisfaction with your current situation. Because, you've forgotten (or never knew) that it was really your job to find God in it and rejoice that He's there, waiting to have you ask Him for a clue, which He'll gladly give you once you remember that He's God and you're not.

Chapter 7 – Job One is Hearing God's Voice

The Shema (Deuteronomy 6:4) is the central prayer of Israel since the days of the Torah. The Torah, which translates to "Teachings," (*not* Law) is comprised of the first five books of the Bible. The Shema is to be recited twice a day; at first light of morning and in the evening. It's probably the first thing a young Jewish boy learns.

Shema Yisrael Adonai Eloheinu Adonai Echad

Hear, O Israel the Lord our God, the Lord is One.

In Hebrew, it looks sort of like this (remember to read from right to left):

שְׁמַע, יִשְׂרָאֵל: יְהוָה אֱלֹהֵינוּ, יְהוָה אֶחָד.

The book of Deuteronomy, in the sixth chapter and seventh verse states that *"these words"* be spoken of *"when you lie down, and when you rise up."* If we are to "hear" God as the Shema proclaims, then that presumes that God has something to say to us and we are, indeed, supposed to be *hearing it*. These words were spoken and written in the time immediately following Israel's freedom from bondage in Egypt.

If you look carefully at the original Hebrew, the word "hear" more fully means to listen intelligently with an attitude directed towards action or obedience. So, in effect, the Shema is saying, *"Listen, Israel..."* Or, *"Hear me and respond..."*

In Deuteronomy we see:

> *"Now, O Israel, **listen** to the statutes and the judgments which I teach you to observe, that you may live, and go in and possess the land which the LORD God of your fathers is giving you"* (Deuteronomy 4:1 NKJV).

Again, we see that we are to **listen,** which means that there must be something we are to hear. As a matter of fact, the word "listen" in this passage is the same word in the original Hebrew as the word "hear" used in the Shema – to listen intelligently, with an intent directed towards action.

> *"One of the teachers of the law came and heard them debating. Noticing that Jesus had given them a good answer, he asked him, "Of all the commandments, which is the most important?" "The most important one," answered Jesus, "is this: 'Hear, O Israel, the Lord our God, the Lord is one'"* (Mark 12:28-29a).

We can feel assured of the strength and the promise that the Shema represents. It's so important and powerful that Jesus claims it as the most important commandment the Lord has given us, and it starts with the command to "hear," "listen," and "act."

The Lord has been taking me on a journey. He's taking you on one, too. During this journey, He has given me dreams – dreams so vivid and real I knew that the Holy Spirit was speaking in and through them. Along the way in that journey, the Lord gave me an adult Sunday

The Alpha Male

School class to serve, and He gave me the word, "Hear." So, I began to read, so that I could find out what He was telling me about this word. I quickly added "listen" to the search list, because it became obvious that listening is a crucial part of hearing. Since I began this search for meaning in the scriptures, I have made a list of over one thousand times that the word listen/hear is used. In the vast majority of cases, the same Hebrew word for both "listen" and "hear" is used in the Old Testament and a very similar or exactly the same meaning is intended in the New Testament. Let's set the stage for the next one. The Lord has just delivered the Ten Commandments through Moses.

> *"When the people saw the thunder and lightning and heard the trumpet and saw the mountain in smoke, they trembled with fear. They stayed at a distance and said to Moses, 'Speak to us yourself and we will listen. But **do not have God speak to us or we will die**'" (Exodus 20:18-19).*

This is where God's chosen people bailed on hearing directly from God. They would listen to Moses…sort of…when convenient. But, listening to God was just a bit too much to ask – pretty scary, even.

In Numbers we see that the Lord hears what we say.

> *"Miriam and Aaron began to talk against Moses because of his Cushite wife, for he had married a Cushite. 'Has the LORD spoken only through Moses?' they asked. 'Hasn't he also spoken through us?' And the LORD heard this" (Numbers 12:1-2).*

Uh-oh, did they think the Lord couldn't hear them, or wasn't really paying attention? Yikes! The Lord called the three out of the tent of meeting and summoned Aaron and Miriam forward. He said:

"**Listen** to my words: When there are prophets of the LORD among you, I reveal myself to them in visions, I speak to them in dreams. But this is not true of my servant Moses; he is faithful in all my house. With him I speak face to face, clearly and not in riddles; he sees the form of the LORD. Why then were you not afraid to speak against my servant Moses?'" (Numbers 12:6-8).

Really good question, that one – *"Why then were you not afraid to speak against my servant Moses?"*

Let's look at a few more important verses that contain the word hear or listen. The two are used pretty much interchangeably in translation, with the same Hebrew word in the original text.

"Come, let us bow down in worship...Today, if only you would **hear** his voice" (Psalm 95:6a, 7b).

"Why spend money on what is not bread, and your labor on what does not satisfy? **Listen, listen to me**, and eat what is good, and you will delight in the richest of fare. Give ear and come to me; **listen, that you may live**" (Isaiah 55:2-3a).

"For when **I called**, no one **answered**, when **I spoke, no one listened. Hear** the word of the LORD..." (Isaiah 66:4b-5a).

"My sheep **listen** to my voice; I know them, and they follow me" (John 10:27).

"Why is my language not clear to you? Because you are unable to hear what I say. You belong to your father, the devil..." (John 8:43-44a).

So, can man hear from God? You'd better believe it. We have the authority of His son, Jesus – Yeshua (in Hebrew). Yeshua is speaking to the gathering that includes a group of Pharisees who were challenging Him on who He is. In the most powerful statement possible on this subject, Jesus tells them:

> *"Whoever belongs to God hears what God says. The reason you do not hear is that you do not belong to God" (John 8:47).*

You cannot get any more plain than that. And, Jesus wasn't talking about hearing as in reading Torah, because ALL of those He was addressing read Torah and could recite all of it to you from memory. As an additional source of authority, let's hear what the Lord says through Isaiah:

> *"When someone tells you to consult mediums and spiritists, who whisper and mutter, should not a people inquire of their God? Why consult the dead on behalf of the living? Consult God's instruction and the testimony of warning" Isaiah 8:19-20a).*

Clearly, if God says that you're to inquire of Him rather than some fortune teller, it means that He will answer you. Therefore, if you're not hearing from God, you need to check in with Jesus and find out why. You probably need to get on your knees and start apologizing – for pride, rebellion, lust of the eye, lust of the flesh, whatever it is that is standing between you and God. It's testifying against you, because that is what it will do. You need to ask for forgiveness and restoration. If you haven't already asked that Jesus be your Lord and forgive you of your sins, then this is absolutely the time to do it. Do it now. He has all the authority to do that. This is not something you want to put off until a rainy day.

"People were eating, drinking, marrying and being given in marriage up to the day Noah entered the ark" (Luke 17:27a).

The day the rain started, Noah closed the Ark.

"...the day Lot left Sodom, fire and sulfur rained down from heaven and destroyed them all" (Luke 17:29).

Natural / Rational Man

The most ridiculous thing rational man can do is to assume that he can search out, and fully comprehend, how and what God thinks, and what He might have to say, without asking Him. Rationality carries the meaning of lucidity – of the ability to make sense of things – to be able to explain, at least to oneself, exactly what's going on. Rationality is likely your biggest obstacle to clearly hearing from God.

God is not subject to "natural law" but is the Creator of it – it's something He *built*. He is not run by it, and is not ever constrained by it. A large percentage of people would probably look sideways at your recounting of Daniel's visions of angels and their descriptions of contending with other spiritual beings, and other angels coming to their aid. Many would probably insist that it was only a dream of Daniel's, or perhaps some hallucinogen that he inadvertently ingested. Our rational minds have a big problem with the concept of celestial beings showing up and talking to us, not to mention the craziness of the Lord God of All Creation having a word with us. Yet, He tells us that's exactly what He does and will keep doing, as long as we want to hear from Him. Yet, again, even after one has pushed God away, sometimes in anger, sometimes in rebellion, He extends the olive branch to us, the prodigal, hoping to bring us back to the fold – the one lost, while the ninety-nine are safe, at home. A marvelous, miraculous

The Alpha Male

God, that behaves in ways we cannot possibly comprehend. Yet, here we are, the recipients of His outpouring of love and blessing. And, we yearn to define Him in earthly terms that we can then explain to ourselves, and then go back to playing video games.

It appears that as we age, we become even more locked onto rationality. Many years of computer systems engineering trained my brain to operate as if *everything* can be explained. Not only can it be explained, it can be planned, prevented, avoided and minutely understood and controlled. There are no mysteries. But, then we have Jesus telling us that *"...anyone who will not receive the kingdom of God like a little child will never enter it" (Luke 18:17)*. I believe that Jesus is telling us that we are not capable of understanding much of what is true regarding the spiritual world, and so we must come as little children, with the expectation of wonderful mysteries that we can't explain, but we love them, anyway. Like children at a magic show, they are delighted to see the magician pull a coin from behind someone's ear. The adults in the crowd know for certain that there is a trick involved and that it can be explained. If you could just get closer you could see what's really going on. After all, everything can be *explained*. While there are some things that may be explained, I'm pretty sure there's a lot about heaven that we cannot fathom in our wildest imagination or with our sharpest brainpower.

Many adults can offer possible explanations for the miracles Jesus performed – you know – scientific, rational explanations that remove the word "miracle" and substitute "trick," "treatment," or "process." The world challenges us to resist miracles, to *not* believe them. Our training tells us that it's a magic act and that we're being played for chumps in some carnival huckster's booth on the midway. But, Jesus tells us that *"...whatever you ask for in prayer, believe that you have received it, and it will be yours" (Mark 11:24)*. Immediately some will jump on this statement and take it to absurdity – the "name it and claim it" crowd is a perfect example. They want to reduce the power of God to a vending machine that only requires that you speak the secret phrase into the microphone to make a wish and see it come true...the Kingdom of God reduced to a fairy tale, complete with a wishing well. Or, just as likely a reaction would be to recount some prayer that was made, to which God seemingly made no response. There was no healing, no saving of a life, or no intervention for that job you wanted so badly. The essence of what they're saying is that God really doesn't answer prayers, or that His answers to prayer were only in the Bible. Perhaps that was only for the apostles. But, I've lived and seen way too many miracles to even temporarily entertain that thought. God penetrates our reality when it pleases Him, or when we're acting in accord to what He wants, and how He wants. Jesus warns us that:

> *"...if you hold anything against anyone, forgive them, so that your Father in heaven may forgive you your sins" (Mark 11:25).*

That forgiveness is supposed to be happening before your request for that miracle – that intervention. That means that there's a connection between your heart and your petition for heavenly intercession in an earthly matter – that miracle *you're* looking for. Are you looking for something that *He* wants, or for something *you* want? If you're looking for something He wants, how do you know He wants it? Did He tell you that He wants it and that you're the only one who has the key that can unlock His power? Probably, not. At the moment when you think that you're the one in charge, your heart has been mugged by your ego and the earthly lust for power just raised its ugly head. But, Jesus had more to say about our ability to ask for heavenly intervention in earthly matters. He was speaking to His gathered disciples only hours before He would go to the cross.

> *"I no longer call you servants, because a servant does not know his master's business. Instead, I have called you friends, for everything that I learned from my Father I have made known to you. You did not choose me, but I chose you and appointed you so that you might go and bear fruit—fruit that will last—and so that whatever you ask in my name the Father will give you"* (John 15:15-16).

So, *that* is a more complete explanation of praying for miracles. For one, it means that when you ask for something, you ask because you know that's what He wants. Secondly, you ask in the name of Jesus – acting on behalf of Jesus – to His Heavenly Father – *your* Heavenly Father – because you're Jesus' friend and you know what He wants. Then, the Father will give it to you. That's a pretty important distinction in the quality level of what we might pray for.

> *"You desire but do not have, so you kill. You covet but you cannot get what you want, so you quarrel and fight. You do not have because you do not ask God. When you ask, you do not receive, because you ask with wrong motives, that you may spend what you get on your pleasures"* (James 4:2-3).

Is it to fulfill an earthly desire we have for *things*? Or, is it a heavenly desire that brings glory to the Kingdom? I don't know about you, but that just wiped out almost all the things on my prayer list regarding *things*. Most of what's left is about the needs of those around me, very often related to physical healing from disease, or spiritual and physical damage. I include emotional damage under spiritual because our emotions can drag down our spirit and force it into subservience. Then, bad things happen.

Physicists tell us that there are many more dimensions than those we can experience and comprehend – somewhere between ten and twenty-six of them, depending on which theory you might support. One can sit in a modern college physics class and hear this sort of conversation with a detached objectivity, pretending we can imagine twenty-six dimensions, and then we turn around and try to limit God to only moving in four of them. The bottom line is that God wants to talk to you, and He wants you to talk to Him. Get ready to hear from God in a language you can understand. If your parent needs to tell you something important, they aren't going to tell you in French if you don't speak French. They're going to tell you in a language that they know you will understand.

> *"Which of you fathers, if your son asks for a fish, will give him a snake instead? Or if he asks for an egg, will give him a scorpion?" (Luke 11:11-12a).*

In my own life, I recall that many of my most energetic conversations with God have been when I was mad at Him about something. It's a painful remembrance that I have let my negative emotions monopolize my most heartfelt conversations with the King of Glory. And, yet, He still talks to me. What a magnificent, loving God He is to be so generous, so kind, so forgiving that He lets me behave like a brat toddler not getting his way, while He is the patient parent, wanting what is best for me, and loving me through it all. I'm sure He would like to see me grow up a little quicker. God knows that you struggle with your humanity. He invites you to untie your mind/spirit from physical reality and step into Kingdom thinking and seeing – beyond even those numerous dimensions you may have heard about in physics class.

How Do We Listen For God's voice?

To hear, we must stop talking. You can't listen when you're talking and you can't hear without listening. Get into a listening position, mentally. Praise and worship invite our hearts to soften so that we can get into a frame of mind wherein we *can* listen. Turn off the hum and static of the world. Tune into the clear channel of God's transmission into our hearts. Start off with reading your Bible. Just open it up to some unknown spot and put your finger down and read. The Lord knows exactly how to speak to a heart that's ready to hear. Start thinking and acting like a friend of God, rather than as a piece of human debris that is stinking up His palace. He wants you to Kingdom-think – to see the world through the lens of eons-on-their-way-to-eternity, rather than mere weeks or even your own physical lifespan. He wants you to see the world as a Son or Daughter of the Most-High God of all Creation – HaShem – The Name – Elohim – The Supreme God – I AM. Then, you can more properly hear what He's saying. It's important because if you are expecting Him to talk to you about mindless things, you're tuned into the wrong channel. What's important to God? Well, for starters, His children. He loves them. He wants you to love them. He wants you to carry the Good News to them that will save them from that day when they'll answer for their lives and who they claim as their Lord and Savior. He wants you to snatch them from the fire. So, as you get used to the idea of listening, then you may begin to hear.

> *"Do not merely listen to the word, and so deceive yourselves. Do what it says. Anyone who listens to the word but does not do what it says is like someone who looks at his face in a mirror and, after looking at himself, goes away and immediately forgets what he looks like. But whoever looks intently into the perfect law that gives freedom, and continues in it—not forgetting what they have*

heard, but doing it—they will be blessed in what they do" (James 1:22-25).

Probably the most effective method for hearing God's voice is to ask Him for His opinion about a specific situation. Ask Him about that job offer. Ask Him about that girl. Ask Him about your life – your thoughts, your habits. If it has been quite a while since you tried to have a conversation with God, there may be some other things He'd like to talk about, first. Be ready to listen and to hear. After really listening and really hearing, then "do." Wait. How do you know you really heard? Ask for confirmation. But, don't take confirmation as some broad category of action or event, like "if the sun comes up tomorrow, then God must want me to do this." Get real and be real with confirmation. If you don't get it, back up and ask again, waiting longer this time to both listen and hear.

Much of what God has to say to us is in the form of "revelation." Revelation means that it is being revealed to you. It's something that has always been true. It didn't just happen or suddenly come into being at this moment. It has been true since God laid the foundation for all creation. You just really saw it for the first time. You may not even get the full import or dynamics of what you've just seen, but you've tuned in like a radio receiver to a message that was sent from before the beginning of time.

Can Satan Fake God's Voice? How Do We Know It's Him?

When we listen for God's voice, how do we know it's Him? First of all, we must rely on the Holy Spirit. But, even more so, we must make certain that we belong to Jesus, for only then can we be assured that we're hearing His voice.

"The one who enters by the gate is the shepherd of the sheep. The gatekeeper opens the gate for him, and the sheep listen to his voice. He calls his own sheep by name and leads them out...and his sheep follow him because they know his voice. But they will never follow a stranger; in fact, they will run away from him because they do not recognize a stranger's voice" (John 10:2-3, 4b-5).

Satan (HaSatan in Hebrew) means "the accuser." His most powerful tool is deception. He deceives those who cannot or, by their own choice will not recognize his activities. So, can Satan fake God's voice? Jesus says no – not to His sheep. He says *"they will run away from him because they do not recognize a stranger's voice."* But, Jesus is referring only to His sheep – those who follow Him and know His voice.

"...Satan himself masquerades as an angel of light. It is not surprising, then, if his servants masquerade as servants of righteousness" (2 Corinthians 11:14-15a).

Praying to the Idol, and Other Grand Mistakes

This was Balaam's problem. Remember Balaam? He was a "diviner," or prophet, who was not Jewish as far as we know, but we know that he did hear from God. Recall that prophecy means to speak on behalf of God. Mr. Balak, King of Moab, was really worried about all those Israelites showing up in his neighborhood. He was so worried about them that he wanted to hire Balaam to come speak curses on them so that he could then defeat them in battle, knowing *"...that whoever you bless is blessed, and whoever you curse is cursed" (Numbers 22:6).* Apparently, Balaam's blessings and curses already had somewhat of a reputation. Balaam started out on the right foot, refusing to curse

God's people. But, Mr. Balak kept offering even more riches each time he asked.

> *"Although Balak were to give me his house full of silver and gold, I could not go beyond the command of the Lord my God, to do less or more" (Numbers 22:18).*

But, Balaam kept looking for a way to get around the Lord's rebuke of what he was trying to do, so that he could satisfy Balak and thereby cash in on those great riches for himself. Balaam was studying the fine print for a way around what God had told him, which was that Balaam was not to curse the Israelites because they were blessed by the Lord God. Balaam began to shift his requests for an answer to his problem – from asking God, to asking Balak's wallet. Praying to the idol means that we are tempted to pray to whatever gives us the answer we want to hear. Balaam had been pretty solid until the price was raised high enough that it got to "an offer he couldn't refuse." Praying to the wallet finally worked and Balaam got the answer he wanted to hear. King Balak had won – the idol (Balak's wallet) that Balaam had been praying to came through for him. It had stopped up his ears and his conscience so that Balaam could ignore what God was telling him. Balaam eventually told Balak that the Israelites could be weakened by getting them to eat meat that was sacrificed to idols and tempting them with sexual immorality. Because, then their conscience would testify against them and proclaim them guilty before God. Some would repent and be restored. The others would run and hide.

> *"But I have a few things against you: you have some there who hold to the teaching of Balaam, who taught Balak to put a stumbling block before the people of Israel, so that they would eat food sacrificed to idols and practice fornication" (Revelation 2:14 NRSV).*

So, Balaam eventually gave Balak what he wanted, and for that Balaam received riches at the hand of King Balak, and helped bring down Israel once again. If you want something badly enough, your desire for it can become the idol you're praying to, and you'll usually get the answer you want…from the idol. So, what we can expect is that Satan will attempt to counterfeit God's voice, and will lie to us. If we decide to deceive ourselves and, like Balaam, try to go around what God answered, then we will find ourselves getting the answer we want instead of God's. So, whatever we hear, whether from man or spirit, must be judged against what we know to be the truth revealed in God's word, and the testimony of the Holy Spirit in our spirit. That is our standard of truth and whatever doesn't measure up against that truth must be discarded as lies, told for our destruction.

Counterfeiting Holiness

Just as Jesus was tempted by Satan, we will be also. Just as Jesus heard from the Father, we will too, through His Holy Spirit. For us to know what God would have us do on this earth, we must tune our hearts to sing His praises and to hear and know what He would have us do. It doesn't matter what the question is – where we live, where we worship, where we invest our time and our resources, or who we let close to us and our family. We need to hear His opinion on the matter.

> *There is a way that seems right to a man, But its end is the way of death" (Proverbs 16:25 NKJV).*

> *"But the natural man does not receive the things of the Spirit of God, for they are foolishness to him; nor can he know them, because they are spiritually discerned" (1 Corinthians 2:14 NKJV).*

Jesus Himself warns that there is a time coming:

John H. Ingle

"For there shall arise false Christs, and false prophets, and shall shew great signs and wonders; insomuch that, if it were possible, they shall deceive the very elect" (Matthew 24:24 KJV).

For starters, note that Jesus is saying that it's *not* possible to deceive the elect, but if it were, this would be the time. Jesus is warning here of those "last days" during which false Christs will appear performing miracles and that even true Christians will *almost* be deceived. It is hard for the human mind to imagine this staggering level of almost overwhelming deception. Whether we are living in the beginnings of the last days is not something I can verify, but the warning is there against the deception of the accuser – HaSatan. One of these false Christs will, of course, be satan himself. For every truth of the Bible, satan has or will have, a counterfeit "truth" in the world. Right now he's trying to undermine the world with a flood of counterfeit Alpha Males. In other matters, he has given the world counterfeits that are so close to the genuine, so close to Bible truth that millions of people are fooled and deceived. He has used this technique very successfully in the past, is using it today, and will use it in the future to deceive the entire world. Satan is going to counterfeit the return of Christ, and millions will be deceived because they have not studied the Bible and aren't hearing His voice. They won't be able to recognize the counterfeit. Instead, they have listened to false teachers who preach a lukewarm and powerless "gospel" that saves no one, or a gospel that gives them power over the deceived. They are helping to prepare the world to accept satan's greatest counterfeit. These will be pretty scary times for those without preparation.

"Not everyone who says to me, 'Lord, Lord,' will enter the kingdom of heaven... Then I will tell them plainly, 'I never knew you'" (Matthew 7:21a, 23a).

"The only thing more important than knowing God is that He knows you" (Bill Johnson, Senior Pastor of Bethel Church, Redding, Ca).

In Luke 13 we are reminded that the devil is the cause of pain and suffering.

"And, behold, there was a woman who had a spirit of infirmity eighteen years, and was bent over, and could in no way raise herself up" (Luke 13:11 NKJV).

Jesus explains who did this to the woman.

"And ought not this woman, a daughter of Abraham whom Satan bound for eighteen long years, be set free from this bondage on the sabbath day?" (Luke 13:16 NRSV).

Now, exactly how Satan did this, we don't know and we're not given any details of how it happened. But, we do know that he did it. We also know that Jesus overruled him.

"For we wrestle not against flesh and blood, but against principalities, against powers, against the rulers of the darkness of this world, against spiritual wickedness in high places" (Ephesians 6:12 KJV).

The earth and its inhabitants started out very different than they are now, through the destructive and deceptive acts of satan. Many who are alive today think that at Judgment Day there is going to be a jury trial and that they will call witnesses who will say that they're a "good person." They paid all their taxes on time and they contributed to saving the whales. They may claim that even you approved of their lifestyle – that you said it was fine, even wonderful - praiseworthy.

After all, that's what you were taught in school, right? Everyone is the same? We all get a participation trophy? We're all good people? There is no such thing as sin? Is it just a matter of different perspectives?

But, God doesn't use juries. He is the final arbiter of your eternity and you don't get to call witnesses who excused your rejection of Him. The Lord God is the Alpha and Omega, the First and the Last. There is no opportunity for you to plead your case – your life is the open book that *literally* testifies against you. Your imperfect life is speaking for you and your voice is silenced. But, the Good News for you is that if Jesus is your attorney, He can plead your case. He can turn to the Father, and say, "Oh, look, here's Johnny's name in the Book of Life. I paid his tab, already. Welcome, Johnny! Come on in and let me show you around."

Temptations abound in nearly every facet of life – the temptation to have sex outside of marriage; to tell partial truths in order to coerce someone into doing something which benefits oneself; the temptation to take something home of your employer's, because "they have plenty"; the temptation to skim money from a business operation – the list is endless, and the excuses we come up with are endless and always very rational sounding. The myth (provided by the evil one) is that "you're a good person," so that you now have excuses for every bad behavior in your entire life – you just have to have someone around who approves of what you're doing. It is an evil myth. Unrepentant bad behavior is a huge blockade to hearing God's voice. So, if you're not hearing it, start there. There's an old military saying – *"In war the first casualty is the truth."* We are in a war and the only place you'll get truth is from God. Any other source is suspect and likely false. Good pastors can help you reveal truth in the Word, but they can't replace hearing from God. They can't hear Him for you. Your believing friends will often share with you what they are hearing from

God, as well. But, believing *them* (or me) should not be automatic. As the Bible tells us, "Test the spirits."

> *"Dear friends, do not believe every spirit, but **test the spirits** to see whether they are from God, because many false prophets have gone out into the world" (1 John 4:1).*

Chapter 8 – A Tale of Two Alpha Males

Let's look at a couple of Alpha Males from the Bible and see what we can learn from their character and their lives. God chose each young man for different reasons and used their very different talents exactly the way He wanted. By far, two of the most fascinating fully mortal young men in the Bible are Joseph and David.

The Life of Joseph

We meet Joseph at the tender young age of 17, and hear that he had been out with his brothers, tending the sheep, and brought his father a bad report about his brothers. That scorecard he kept on his brothers was probably a good indication of how his relationship went with them. Joseph was one of the two youngest sons of Jacob. Both of them were born to him by his wife, Rachel. Rachel was Jacob's favorite wife. Jacob was pretty fond of Joseph and the Bible even tells us that Joseph was his favorite because he was born during Jacob's old age. Jacob even went so far as to give Joseph a very ornate coat – often referred to as a "coat of many colors." This made it pretty obvious to all the brothers that Dad had a soft spot for Joseph that exceeded what they thought might extend to them.

The Alpha Male

Imagine for a moment: Joseph comes bounding downstairs for breakfast, yawning, stretching and looking for food. His brothers are their usual surly and sullen selves that morning, bordering on open anger. While rummaging through the pantry, he turns and says to his brothers, "Oh, Hey! I had a dream last night that you guys were all bowing down to me." At that point Joseph's brothers were fully on their way to ticked off. Imagine the nerve of a very much younger brother suggesting that he's going to have you bowing down before him. They probably wanted to kill him about then. Oh, hey, wait! They were about to try and do just that! Fortunately for Joseph, one of his older brothers understood the folly of that project and stayed in between him and his brothers for the next several, fun adventures they were about to have.

Joseph was about to become as alone as a young Jewish boy could possibly be. You have to wonder how he continued in the promise that God had showed him. God had a plan and would not be prevented from accomplishing it. When Joseph was sold into slavery by his brothers and taken to a very foreign land, how did he keep it together? Was he able to get support and encouragement from all his other Jewish buddies at weekly Shabbat services or at their usual Wednesday night prayer group meeting? Mmm…no. There weren't any other Jewish buddies and his support group consisted of fellow slaves being auctioned off at the marketplace.

Joseph seemed to catch a break and became Potiphar's house servant but then Potiphar's wife accused him of sexual assault when he didn't want to party with her. Joseph is sent to prison with still no spiritual support outside his relationship with God. While in prison Joseph interpreted dreams for two of his cellmates but his help was soon forgotten. You can almost hear his cellmates telling him, "Yeah, Joseph, that dream sure seems to be working out well for you. You can almost see the stars and sheaves bowing down to you here in this smelly, rotten prison cell. Yeah, you just keep on believing that stuff about heavenly favor."

Regardless of how hopeless matters might have looked to him at any one moment, Joseph persisted in performing with excellence. He believed God that the promise – that vision – which God had shown him, would come to pass, regardless of what may try to present itself as master over his situation. God was the real master and Joseph believed God. God presented Joseph to the king at the exact moment He had prepared for Joseph to assume the role that was meant for him, all along. Joseph wasn't just the Alpha Male and leader of his family. He became the leader of all of Egypt, answering only to the king. Joseph had been remarkably patient – almost unbelievably so. Remember, though, that God loves it when we believe Him, even though it looks impossible. Faith combined with persistence is faithfulness. Remember what happened with Abraham, when he *"believed God?" "It was counted unto him as righteousness."* What does it mean to "Believe God?" It means to count on Him. It means to trust Him with everything about your existence – what you'll eat, where you'll go, why you'll be there. Why does He do that? Because He wants us to trust Him and know Him as Creator, *"Father of Lights, in whom is no shadow of turning."* That's our faith in action – believing Him and not backing down from the promise. Joseph is the poster boy for hearing from God, or at least he was in a close tie with the prophet Daniel. Joseph showed extraordinary skills in organization and leadership during difficult times of famine and death and the tribes of Israel would remember his role in it. Their very lives would depend on it.

The Life of David

In my personal opinion, David is the most thoroughly interesting person we're given in the Bible. He is a person of such strength, persistence, and wit that we have to shake our heads at the thought of his missteps. The Lord likes him a lot; so much so that he chose David's lineage to carry His own, to establish His own, eternal throne through him:

> *"For to us a child is born, to us a son is given...He will reign on David's throne and over his kingdom, establishing and upholding it with justice and righteousness from that time on and forever" (Isaiah 9:6a, 7b).*

From reading about his life, I would venture to say that David was probably a pretty fun guy to be around. He was smart, witty, joyful, and he loved the Lord. David was an Alpha Male. We first get to know David in the Bible through an event most everyone has heard about. David came to visit his brothers and bring them food at a stand-off between the army of Israel and the army of the Philistines. The Philistines' challenge to Israel was to send out one man to fight to decide which army will be servants and which army is master. While David was in the camp he heard Goliath shouting his challenge, again, to the army of Israel and wanted to know why nothing was being done about it. David went to Saul to volunteer to fight him but Saul told him he was too young and inexperienced. David told him:

> *"Your servant has killed both the lion and the bear; this uncircumcised Philistine will be like one of them, because he has defied the armies of the living God" (1 Samuel 17:36).*

Saul saw the intensity and determination in David and so he relented and told David to wear Saul's own personal armor, but it was too large and heavy. Note that the "armor" didn't fit his body and it didn't fit his gifts. When he put aside man's idea of how to deal with Goliath he quickly turned back to the skills and knowledge God had already given him. Goliath became headless compost and David became a celebrated hero of Israel.

After his victory over Goliath, King Saul knew that the Lord was with David. Saul proceeded to give him all sorts of errands and missions. David did everything that was asked and was successful in all that he did.

> *"In everything he did he had great success, because the* LORD *was with him"* (1 Samuel 18:14).

This didn't sit very well with Saul because Saul thought that he was the one calling all the shots, not God, and certainly not David. His jealousy of David grew, quickly. Saul was *not* the Alpha Male, but he played one, for a time. Saul was fearful and couldn't remember who his daddy was. David held his tongue and controlled himself. David now knew he would ascend to the throne, but backed away carefully from any opportunity to accelerate that process. Saul tried to kill him on multiple occasions. When Saul and his army were pursuing David, he slipped into their camp and stood over Saul's sleeping body. David could have run Saul through with a spear while he slept, but he knew that God didn't want that, and had great respect for *"God's Anointed."* God wanted David to stick to His plan and His timing. To his credit, David stuck to God's way of doing it. However, in the meantime, Saul pursued David relentlessly to kill him in a hopeless attempt to save his own throne.

For a time David felt like there was no place for him and he began to feel that he could no longer hear God's voice and he feared for his life.

The Alpha Male

At one point his entire family had been captured by the Amalekites but God assured him that they would recover everyone and all his property without harm. And, they did. David's life as King is accounted for in great detail in the Bible. His life was a testimony for all his people and his Psalms and prayers are read daily by believers all around the world, today. But, there were moments in his life of really bad decisions – decisions so bad that it cost him and his country, dearly. But, God's purpose prevailed in David's life.

There is freedom in worship – in being able to freely praise our Heavenly Father without regard for anything, or for anyone's opinion. You don't have to be in a church building to do that. David's worship delighted the Lord, I think, because it was so freely and so frequently given. When King David danced in the street in praise, his wife took offense and pitched a fit. She didn't think he was acting "kingly" enough to suit her and the reputation she had in mind to maintain. She seemed to be dwelling on appearances – on pleasing men – and she must not have thought he was making a very good one. But, he was The King, worshipping the King of Kings, so her ill-advised commentary on his public behavior cost her, enormously. He assessed her condemnation of his actions as being so far out of her place that he punished her. Her role in the increase of his kingdom would die with her in her solitude. Her ill-advised commentary was…well…ill-advised.

David's song and verse are a source of refuge and inspiration that staggers the mind in its breadth and its power. His capacity for praise of the Lord God is an example for every believer.

> *"Yet you are holy, enthroned on the praises of Israel. In you our ancestors trusted; they trusted, and you delivered them. To you*

they cried, and were saved; in you they trusted, and were not put to shame" (Psalm 22:3-5 NRSV).

David practically invented praise and worship on behalf of the Lord. The Book of Psalms is the most complete book of praise and thanksgiving that you will ever find. And, no doubt the Lord was pained by David's grievous acts. His selfishness at moments was as bad as our own.

In a sense, man is a dangerous animal – no doubt, the most dangerous. David spoke of having to kill both the lion and the bear while defending his flock. To the lion and the bear that died at his hands, David was a pretty dangerous fellow. But, if you study the Bible enough you begin to see that the men of the Bible are "everyman," much like you and me. Their advantages and strengths are God-given, and each of them was unique. Both their greatest victories and most ignominious failures are found there in raw, open display. Those men are there as examples to us, of both their greatness through Him, and their failures when they ignored his leading and were overcome by their selfish desires. But, both David and Joseph were Alpha Males and showed extraordinary tenacity in holding onto God's promises.

Chapter 9 – Outsourcing God

"In countries which have fallen under communist rule, it is often the Church which forms the most powerful barrier against a completely totalitarian system. And, so, totalitarian regimes always seek either to destroy the Church, or, when that is impossible, to subvert it." Ronald Reagan

A Nation of Sheep

In a minefield, it's good to know where the mines are. You are definitely in a minefield. It's populated by a world of largely confused and deceived people. While the political spectrum is full of theater that can hypnotize the masses, it's helpful if we remain aware of the tools that are being used against us. Christians have largely run from dealing with the political arena in the same way they've run from show business and the media. Most of the watching world is seeing only one viewpoint of the universe every day. Meanwhile, the deception of the masses is moving forward at a breathtaking rate. It is astounding how many young people have been talked into embracing the concept that there are many more than two genders, and that you get to decide yours.

John H. Ingle

The Western world, especially the United States, has become a nation of followers. They have been raised and trained to do what someone else wants them to do. That someone is usually government or its favorite tool, "education." I've found that they are generally not aware of it. The primary goal of education has become training and indoctrination, and *not* education. Training is what you get when you need to learn how to do a repetitive task – stick this part into that part and turn that screw. Education is for learning how to think critically, and evaluate both the cause and effect of an action, perhaps without even having to do it. Doing a repetitive task makes you valuable to an employer who doesn't really care if you think or not. Thinking goes along with studying. Thinking is what you do when you make decisions about how you want to: spend your life; who you want to marry; what you want your kids to see and hear. You can count on being "trained" to do whatever modern society and the government think is best for them, for their own gain. Amidst whatever society and the government are doing, you can be sure that evil is alongside to steer the way to somewhere else that isn't being advertised.

Training young people to be compliant and obedient means that the government gets to do largely whatever it wants. After all – who knows better than the government? The government knows everything! The challenge for the Alpha Male is to manage to get through the "training" process with his head on straight. Many parents in the busy pace of modern life have turned over the task of education to the public schools. The public schools have been taken over by the Federal government, and a whole host of people who think it's more important that you learn that there are 40 genders, and that sexual relations between adults and children is natural. If they're taught to think then they will immediately understand that neither of those is true. This change in the schools has been going on for decades – slowly at first. Now, it is accelerating and it's becoming more obvious that it can be used as a tool of indoctrination that typically is not in your best interest.

Government is not your friend and it was never supposed to be. All of these people working for the government are supposed to be your employees, not your masters. The highest governmental authority in the land is the Constitution, not the House of Representatives, or the President. Government is supposed to be a servant of the citizenry, at least in the United States. But, it's not necessarily a well-behaved servant.

> *"Government is not reason, it is not eloquence, it is force; like fire, a troublesome servant and a fearful master. Never for a moment should it be left to irresponsible action."* - - *George Washington*

Unfortunately, we now live in an age when government has largely been left to irresponsible action, and it strongly craves to be the master. The nation has been dumbed down (trained) to now behave essentially as helpless androids that are dependent upon the government and social media. Vast numbers of young people come out of high school knowing how to use their smartphones to stay in touch with every facet of social media, but without much smarts about how to think. Mostly, they react, without thinking, and they depend upon their feelings for their morals, direction and grounding. Probably the worst guide you can use in life is feelings. Feelings are transitory and change by the day with one's life experiences and exposure to the ideas and guidance of others who may not have your best interest in mind. Who is surprised that the youth of this nation are so badly prepared to make the staggeringly important life choices before them?

John H. Ingle

Educating Young Alpha Males and Brides

With government-run schools we have two problems. The first is that they are run by the government. Your taxes fund their existence, yet you have very little to say about what is taught to your children. Christians are essentially being double-taxed if they choose to homeschool or send their children to a private school. I believe it's time for a groundswell of Christians and agreeable non-Christians to make vouchers the law of the land. Vouchers enable parents to send their children to the school of their choice. Your tax dollars then follow your children to whatever school you choose. The strong anti-Christian, secular forces that dominate the present education system seem to grow stronger by the day. They have to have their power in our children's lives severely reduced, if not eliminated entirely. These highly organized devotees have a drawer full of reasons and excuses why you cannot touch the sanctity of public schools. Regardless of what argument they might put forward, what your children learn and see every day in their education is so important that it has to be done. Every day that passes brings us a new example of how public schools have gotten completely out of control with the power they extend into our homes.

The second problem of having government-run schools is that every alternative is extremely expensive. For families that are already having a hard time making ends meet, the added cost of either homeschooling or a Christian school is practically insurmountable. They're already paying for public schools through taxes. To add the cost of an alternative to the top of that pile is too much. I've had my sons in either homeschools or Christian schools in multiple times through their education years as the need was seen. When there was no money for Christian schools we homeschooled them. Yes, it was hard – really hard. Fortunately, the boys were young enough to not understand yet

The Alpha Male

how poor we were. We also lived on acreage out in the countryside, so they had cheap adventures every day. Operating a household on only one income in today's world can be pretty painful, if not impossible for many. We didn't see any other choice, so we did what we had to do. Through various career changes and large amounts of self-study, I was able to significantly improve my income to the point that we were able to send them, as needed, to a Christian school.

Operating a high quality school environment without a single dime of taxpayer money is very difficult. It typically means that the people that staff it make less than their public school counterparts. Public school teachers are not well known for the competitive wages they earn, so you can see that teaching and operating a high quality Christian school has to be a labor of love for those that do it. And, it still is not affordable for many families that badly need it. I'm not going to attempt to lay out a detailed program for how we can make vouchers a reality. That job belongs to someone else. But, understanding the need and assembling the political will to do it will have an enormous impact on the ability of Christian schools to expand and thrive. The alternative is that our children spend most of their young lives being taught by people that could very well be acting in direct opposition to what you're teaching your children at home. They have your children more than you do. We can't afford not to make this change.

In addition to slashing the power of the government in your children's education, the Church is going to have to step up its determination in education. The Church is going to need to take a close look at how we can contribute to the education of children. This is going to be a big challenge. The average child's life is already pretty full of activities. During the school year they are effectively under the control of the public school system for most of their waking hours. The time that remains is divided up between meals, personal hygiene, travel, and the small gaps in between activities that are hard to use productively because they are small, unpredictable, and hard to use effectively. The Church still has the weekends to contribute to their lives. We can use that time to do things that don't get done, presently. For example, the Church might offer classes in Hebrew and Greek language and their cultures. This would give our children a much greater appreciation for Bible reading and contribute to their understanding of the environment in which the Bible was written. This is only one example. Smart leaders in the Church Body can surely recommend other ways to positively contribute to our children's education, outside of the grasp of secular government.

The Baby Mama Solution

The phenomenon of the "baby mama" is a somewhat recent social abnormality that can be attributed to the lack of the ability to think. Young, high school age girls, thrashing about in their confusion about who they are and what they're doing, suddenly and completely solve all their questions about life by just having a baby. Now, they have a purpose. Now, they have something to do. The fact that they are in no way prepared for that awesome responsibility doesn't occur to them at all. Their ability to think and to make rational decisions about life choices and their consequences has been totally squashed by government-run "education," and a severe lack of spiritual guidance. And, they surely don't know what the Alpha Male looks like. But, they *have* dealt with that whole biological imperative thing we talked about earlier. They are now a parent – often, all by themselves. Oh, they may have relatives to help out – mom steps in, or grandmother steps in. But, they usually don't have a union – a *unity* – between a real man and a real woman, in marriage.

That union of marriage is the cauldron in which most of us will be stirred in life, to learn, adapt and grow, and raise our children with that new knowledge and wisdom that is gained from living in a marriage. We are forced to think, but with such bad preparation as most receive, the early years of marriage can be very rough, and often end in divorce. Baby mama is once again on her own, looking for a substitute husband – one with seemingly no opinions of his own about how she should live her life, because he's not planning on staying. Following the 2008 elections we met "Julia," the government's quasi-female baby mama, who has no man in her life except for the government. If you missed Julia, go look her up – she's a real piece of work. Julia, now with children and no husband, looks to that combined husband, father, government figurehead to solve all her problems – that government that is "a force, like fire."

Where does all this leave the struggling, emerging Alpha Male, still mired in our government process of "education?" For starters, it should leave him very distrustful of looking to government to solve *any* of his problems. The Alpha Male must be free – it is in his DNA – it's how God made him. So, how will he allow himself to be enslaved? 2 Peter 2:19 tells us:

> *"(The wicked) promise them freedom, while they themselves are slaves of depravity—for 'people are slaves to whatever has mastered them.'"*

So, where is freedom? It is in the Father. We absolutely must hear His voice.

Like a Moth to a Flame

I'm drawn to political discussion and positions like a moth to flame. I have a great affection for our Constitution and the men who framed it.

John H. Ingle

I am very fond of this country and I've been too frequently irritated by those who don't value it or the lives of the men who fought and died to create it and keep it for us. I honor the men who have fought, been maimed, and have died in the wars that have kept us free as a country. I've lamented those same losses when those men suffered and many gave their all for some ignorant and very temporary political position. I've argued to protect the state of our culture, our society, our highest aspirations, and our sanctity before God, whom we serve. I have been concerned for the image that we present to the world of the God we worship – the Uncreated God – The First and the Last – the God of all Creation. I have lobbied for the best face we can offer, and try to argue eloquently, to help our side win in the courts of public opinion. In the meantime God has been going about His business.

I've been busy…as busy as Martha was in the story told about her in the Book of Luke…as busy as a spring day. But I had no fruit to show for that valiant exertion of my will on my environment. I have railed against those who would corrupt our country, debasing it before all of God's Creation – this magnificent gift we've chanced upon like some incredible winning lottery ticket we've been born into. I could just as easily have been born in some arid wasteland and died young of dysentery. But, as the years crept by, I began to feel a greater tug of the Spirit, and the gnawing feeling that I was wasting my time and His. With a sense of some desperation, I asked the Holy Spirit that He show me REAL – that He show me the value of what I do and tell me whether it looks anything like what He would have me doing. And, He has shown me. He told me that I've been wasting my time. He put the Bible in front of me and talked to me about the fig tree that bears no fruit. Fortunately for me He didn't also tell me that I would never bear fruit again. What He did tell me though, is that I had been trying to fix man's world with man's tools – a losing proposition if there ever was one. He also told me that I was worrying about the outside of the cup – cleaning it so as to be beautiful, but inside it is full of death…just as He had told the Pharisees.

So, I had to stop and admit that to struggle to arrive through the ballot box to a destination that can't be reached by the work of a man's hands, is foolishness. I've been expecting the fix the world so that it would behave as if they are redeemed through the power of God. But, if not, we'll at least make them act like believers by the laws of the land. There I am, trying to protect God's Kingdom and Lordship from the opinions of the world. Such vanity and misdirection can only come from the reasoning of men. The Lord God says, *"Not by Might, Not by Power, But by My Spirit."* Okay, I had been running too frequently on the wrong track. I had to ask, "Now what?"

God sat me down and put before me His Word regarding the reprobate mind – unable to see, hear or grasp what is before it – because the owner of that mind has (while in full command of their rational faculties) refused to allow the knowledge of God to exist alongside their other thoughts. I think that, largely, it's just too inconvenient for many people to not be the master of everything around them. Or, at least to pretend that's the situation. If God isn't there, then man can be the master, instead of the servant. How can I raise myself up above those around me if I have to acknowledge the magnificence of God next to my supposed righteousness that actually smells like death and looks like filthy rags when I operate without God in my life? So, God gives those who knowingly reject Him, as their reward, over to a reprobate mind, where they no longer have to fight against Him or the Creation that testifies to His Lordship over it all. I was in awe and a bit terrified. But, I found myself pulled back to the beginning, to say:

John H. Ingle

"For I am not ashamed of the gospel of Christ, for it is the power of God to salvation for everyone who believes..." (Romans 1:16 NKJV).

That is the truth on this earth that keeps me seeking God in my life. I was driving down the highway one day in 2015 and I found myself talking to God. Actually, He was talking to me. I was mostly listening. I had been pondering all the social and legal upheaval that's been happening and had been asking Him how I should respond to it all. He suddenly began answering me. He said, "The house is on fire and your task is to lead people out of the fire, to safety." My mind quickly began to visualize the dangerous act of going into a burning house and He said, "The fire won't harm you." Okay, that sounded good. He continued, "You keep trying to save the house. It can't be saved. It will be ashes and there's nothing you can do to stop that. I need you to lead people out of the house, to safety." I didn't really feel like this was a good time to ask a lot of questions, such as, "When will it be ashes?" I felt like that wasn't any of my business, and that there was a bigger picture here that was much more serious. Besides, I was in a mild state of shock. I did ask Him later about "the house." He said that, "The house is what man has built." Again, I didn't ask Him to elaborate on exactly what that meant, as I assumed that what man has built is a pretty broad topic, and that it was *all* going to be less than ashes.

A few days later, I asked the Lord to give me a word of confirmation, as well as a clue as to what I might say to others about this encounter. He told me to pick up my Bible, open it with my thumbnail, drop my finger onto a verse, and begin to read:

"But, dear friends, remember what the apostles of our Lord Jesus Christ foretold. They said to you, 'In the last times there will be scoffers who will follow their own ungodly desires.' These are the

people who divide you, who follow mere natural instincts and do not have the Spirit. But you, dear friends, by building yourselves up in your most holy faith and praying in the Holy Spirit, keep yourselves in God's love as you wait for the mercy of our Lord Jesus Christ to bring you to eternal life. Be merciful to those who doubt; save others by snatching them from the fire; to others show mercy, mixed with fear—hating even the clothing stained by corrupted flesh" (Jude 1: 17-23).

I was speechless, realizing that of all the Bible verses I could even have randomly put my finger on, I couldn't recall any that talk about saving others "by snatching them from the fire." So, I had no hesitation at all in calling that absolute confirmation of what He had told me. In addition to the big picture about "snatching them from the fire," there was the other piece of the message. It was more sensed than coming in words. I felt Him telling me that it's really important to stay in the Spirit. If you're not in the Spirit, get yourself there as soon as you can because that's the only safe place from which you can operate. It was a very strong and distinct impression.

Recall that the real battle is spiritual – "not against flesh and blood." The first step is to understand that you and everyone around you are targets of those who are working towards this "spiritual utopia" of governmental control of every aspect of your life. In the position they'd like to see you in, you are a victim; you are powerless; your daddy is the government; your life is not your own. But, wait! Are you a believer? If you are, then remember that you were *already* bought with a price!

"'I have the right to do anything...but I will not be mastered by anything. Do you not know that your bodies are temples of the

Holy Spirit, who is in you, whom you have received from God? You are not your own..." (1 Corinthians 6:12a, 19).

So, you're not your own – you belong to God – and you're not for rent or sale. It's that simple. In a world that is becoming more and more soothed, tranquilized, and led like helpless, blind sheep – men – Alpha Males are the ones who historically work towards freedom at the cost of security. Women are more likely to trade freedom *for* security, until they find out what it really means, and that it's not really a trade, at all. Women are to be partially excused for this. After all, their *focus* is on security and nurturing – exactly those traits you want in raising a family. The major element I got from His scripture-based response to my question was to go back to His original instruction – "lead people out of the fire, to safety."

Government as God

Long ago and far away, a group of independent thinkers got together and decided that they really didn't like the Church being a branch of government. Actually, it wasn't all that long ago and the "Church" didn't really even look like a real church. One of the primary reasons the colonists came to America from Europe and the British Isles was for religious freedom. In England, historically, the Monarch (the ruling king or queen) is the Supreme Governor of the Church of England. The Church had worked hard to earn a bad reputation for being the cold and distant handmaiden of government. Extreme dislike for that system would be a strong influence on the government that would be created in the new world of the thirteen colonies, and the kind of role it would play in the lives of the colonists. The new government – the United States of America – that was formed has been under constant attack in recent years to conform to a whole new set of rules, far outside the Constitution and our established legal framework.

The Alpha Male

In the USA, today, the polls, if they can be believed, indicate that more people than ever are turning away from the Church. I think it's just as possible that there have been a lot of people who claimed "church membership" for social and business reasons, who now think it no longer matters, so they stopped pretending. Some "churches" have completely departed from the teachings in the Bible. In the current era we've been taught by the "Modern Church of Hollywood," to welcome the sin that the sinner wants to bring with them into the Church. Bringing the sin with them is a comfort, like a favorite pair of bedroom slippers. It lets them feel welcome and secure in a familiar setting. Then, they have no desire or need to leave the sin behind. It is what connects them to their imagined roots in life, and helps them to feel that they've really always been operating in God's perfect will. It removes any social stigma or the need for repentance or even the blood of Jesus. It makes them feel like they've always been good – even perfect. It does away with guilt and validates one's historical perspective of self and life – I've always been who I am – a "good person" who just needed additional input…maybe some of God's…now and then. It's like having an attorney or a CPA available when needed. Those churches are starting to look a lot like the Church of England, and another branch of the Federal Government, guaranteeing "rights" to its membership. To their shame, according to a 2002 survey of Church of England clergy, a third of them don't believe in the resurrection and only half go along with the virgin birth of Jesus. That's an astounding departure from God's Word for the supposed leadership of Christianity in England. That begs the questions, "What is it that they still *do* believe that the Bible teaches? What are they preaching from the pulpit?"

What we need to understand about all these negative changes in the Church is that this is a carefully laid plan of the evil one. Removing and altering the role and importance of the Holy Spirit produces "believers" who have no root and therefore have a disrupted pathway to hearing God's voice. If miracles of physical and spiritual healing can be made to seem no longer possible, or even just a fantasy, then belonging to a church is not much different than belonging to a gym. Watering down the gospel and weakening churches produces new believers who are powerless and directionless. They are led like sheep to go nowhere and do nothing of any importance. The "Good News" is made to seem as hopeless and useless as the rest of the media's "news." It is a full-on assault to make the Church look like just another hobby you could have, except when the Church practices "hate speech" by quoting God's word.

To have the government become the source of the country's moral direction, and the recipient of glory, honor and praise is to outsource God. Government has now become an idol – a full-on false god. The focus shifts from God to man, but we are forewarned that man – the world – is not the source of heavenly vision or the destination of heavenly praise.

> *"If anyone loves the world, the love of the Father is not in him. For all that is in the world—the lust of the flesh, the lust of the eyes, and the pride of life—is not of the Father but is of the world." (1 John 2:15b, 16 NKJV).*

We have arrived at loving government and the world it yearns to rule. It is the answer to all our questions. Government has become the towering cathedral of modern human secularism. The lack of humility in the U.S. capital is breathtaking. As a result, for decades Christians have been seen to run from both politics and show business as fast as they can. No doubt there is a view that both environments are poisonous or radioactive and will fatally contaminate whoever enters there. The end result is that the lust for power and control has run completely off the rails with very little to stand in its way. The media and Hollywood have become eager and sycophantic servants for those who want to govern based on their appetites. They both act like hyenas following the lions around, waiting and hoping to share in the kill, after the lions have their fill.

The government is happy to insert itself into the vacuum left by a people who are rejecting God. It's always ready to supervise outcomes – picking winners and losers according to their victimhood status, or even better, their pocketbook. It's ready to step into the vault of the heavens and attempt to become God, withholding and bestowing blessings and favor to get what it wants from a sickly and compliant people. At that point, government, itself, begins to look a lot like the Anti-Christ. But, government is just a willing and shallow accomplice, manned by countless individuals caught up in their own fears and lust for money and power. Government is not your friend, and it is not looking out for your best interest.

Solomon Asch Conformity Experiment

In the halls of psychology there are a couple of experiments that stand out as bellwethers of their day, and perhaps even more so as a warning to us, today. One such experiment was Solomon Asch's Conformity experiment in the early 1950's. He took a group of male college students and put them in a room to vote on which pairs of lines on a screen were the same size or different. In the group there were several "stooges" that would purposefully give the wrong answer 75% of the time and one participant that didn't know the rest of them were setting him up to look like an idiot. He was always the last one asked for his opinion, so that he could see how everyone else voted, before he cast his vote. As it turned out, the majority of the time, he would go along with their wrong answer.

In the interview after the experiment, each young man was asked why he so often chose the wrong answer, and his response was a bit shocking. Each young man cited a reason or two for his wrong answers. Either he didn't want to be seen as a troublemaker or "different", or he thought the rest of the group had better information than he had. The desire to be liked and to fit in was stronger than the desire to give the correct answer.

Milgram's Obedience to Authority Experiments

Even more appalling is the outcome of an experiment carried out by Stanley Milgram, a psychologist at Yale University. His focus was the conflict between obedience to authority and one's personal conscience. The experiment began in 1961, almost immediately after Adolph Eichmann was tried for crimes committed during World War II. The purpose of the experiment was to find out how far people would go in obeying instructions from a "superior" or "authority figure" if it involved harming another person. During the war crimes trials many lower level military operatives made the claim that they were just "following orders." To most legal and social observers that simplistic defense was a weak one regarding the horrors of the crimes committed under the authority of the National Socialist Party of Germany. Scientists were intrigued by the claims and wanted to know if there was any truth in them – could people actually be reduced to merely robotic entities "following orders?"

In Milgram's study, a group of participants was hired from the public at large. Each of these paid participants would be paired with another "participant" who was secretly working with the experimenters. The two would draw straws to determine who would be the "learner" and who would be the "teacher." The drawing was rigged. The newly hired participant would always draw the straw that made them the "teacher" and the secret participant would be the "learner." They would be observed by a third person – an actor in a lab coat (indicating his "authority") pretending to be the "experimenter." The "learner" was given a list of word pairs and then was tested to remember the word pairs when he was given only one of the words. When he gave the wrong answer (which was very often) the authority figure would direct the "teacher" to give the "learner" an electric shock through electrodes attached to the "learner's" body. The electric panel was "calibrated" to give somewhere between a mild shock and a potentially deadly shock, according to the panel's labeling. The "teacher" was instructed to increase the voltage each time the "learner" made a mistake. The "learner" was not actually being shocked but would put on a believable show that made the "teacher" believe that there was real suffering involved. When the "teacher" would balk at increasing the voltage the "authority" would escalate the intensity of the demand to administer a higher dose. The final escalation was to tell the "teacher" that they had no choice but to do as ordered, and many would administer what was thought to be a potentially deadly shock.

Milgram summarized his findings in a 1974 article, "The Perils of Obedience," published in Harper's Magazine.

> *"I set up a simple experiment at Yale University to test how much pain an ordinary citizen would inflict on another person simply because he was ordered to by an experimental scientist. Stark authority was pitted against the subjects' [participants'] strongest moral imperatives against hurting others, and, with the subjects'*

John H. Ingle

[participants'] ears ringing with the screams of the victims, authority won more often than not."

Either of these experiments should give one pause to consider how easily people are led like sheep to slaughter, or to the horrors of war crimes. Humans frequently abdicate their position of authority in deciding for themselves what is righteous and what is not, especially among the young who have not come to fully realize consequences in the same way an adult is expected to have done. We see that playing out today in our government and in our schools.

"Yet when a man abdicates, or loses, his right to rule, he - often unknowingly - becomes inadvertently ruled by that which is illegitimate. He is ruled by his circumstances, the people around him, his problems, and the challenges he faces. These things rule him because he has lost sight of his own spiritual authority" (Tony Evans in *Kingdom Man*).

Training for blind obedience is a handy tool for those who would corrupt the morals of a nation. Unquestioning obedience to authority is taught throughout our society; even in the halls of our nation's universities. Instead of being taught to think and evaluate, students are taught to fall into line and submit to peer pressure. Authority figures at the university level become little dictators, while pretending to protect the sanctity of "education." When this kind of power is used for evil purposes, it can be an awful weapon. Mass murder, extermination camps and the fall of nations comes to mind.

The desired end result of controlling people is the suppression of their motivation so that they become dependent on the control and provision of others. If you can remove people's desire to excel and grow, and stamp out that independence, and make them *de*pendent, then you can

The Alpha Male

stamp out the fires of freedom in a nation. Just look at the Soviet Union, whose long-awaited financial collapse was so loud it woke up everyone on the planet. Prior to the onslaught of Communism in Russia, it had been a Christian nation. I've found that vanishingly few people know that fact. Go ahead – ask a dozen people about it and see what they say. Once the Communists had seized control of Russia, they quickly destroyed almost all of the churches, there. A few remained, principally as cultural landmarks to be occupied by government "clergy" – if you can even call them that. Over the following several years as the Soviet Union was created from the sorrow-filled rubble, Christianity was virtually stamped out in the same fashion that Communist China is attempting to do again, today. Religion is anathema to Communism, <u>especially</u> Evangelical Christianity. There is power there that they don't understand and they're very jealous of it, and, afraid. Destroying it becomes a priority and a necessity.

Today's politicians, especially those touting Socialism, want your permission to no longer need your permission. They want to run your life, completely and permanently. They don't want to have to come back, every time they have a good idea about what's good for you to get your vote and your permission to control you in a new fashion. They just want you to be quiet and let their superior intellect, judgment, and "spiritual" awareness act as the rule by which you operate in your life. They want power. They want control. These are not nice people. Their devoted followers are scared people – people who are afraid of their own shadows. Their followers are not afraid to give over control of their lives – they're sold on the idea. In Milgram's experiment, many of them would gladly increase the voltage to whatever point was ordered.

"Do not imagine, comrades, that leadership is a pleasure. On the contrary, it is a deep and heavy responsibility. No one believes more firmly than Comrade Napoleon that all animals are equal. He would be only too happy to let you make your decisions for yourselves. But sometimes you might make the wrong decisions, comrades, and then where should we be?" (Squealer the pig, in "Animal Farm," by George Orwell).

The government is quite sure that they'll do a better job of running your life than you will. That leaves no room for God in your life. The government will now be your decider and provider, if you would only let them. Don't be afraid of them – just know what they're up to so that you aren't pulled into their sick game.

Media – Handmaiden to the Political Machine

The media is a gigantic word and picture machine that continually generates the excitement of disaster and chaos. Its business is trouble, and business is good. Reporting on trouble is its daily bread and butter. With around 7.5 billion people on the planet, somewhere at every micro-moment, 24x7, something is going wrong. Someone is being offended, physically hurt, or dying, or some storm or earthquake has happened, or an awful tour bus crash, or some kind of weather disaster. A hundred years ago, you might hear of a car wreck that happened in a nearby town, or a major earthquake on the other side of the ocean, but today you can hear about every little thing that happens all over the globe at almost every moment, giving one the impression that something bad is always happening, or about to happen – maybe to you. It means that you are surrounded by impending doom. You are always waiting for the news that "it's even worse, this time," and "life is over as we know it." It contributes to the sense of inescapable tragedy that drives our modern cultural vision of life. Life becomes so scary and unpredictable that in our modern culture only "me" matters. This gives rise to the anticipation and expectation of bad things, which increases the general desire among the population to let the government try to control everything that happens. When big, bad things happen, the news of it rapidly covers the globe and the media turns it into a non-stop emergency that keeps their audience glued to their continuous broadcast. It becomes a play-by-play of tragedy and suffering. It doesn't matter what happened or why it happened, increased governmental control is always the answer.

The media's ability to sell advertising airtime is now very robust. Bad things equal big money in selling advertising airtime. For them, it's a bonanza. For us, it's a slide into a mindset that expects assault, loss, heartache, damage, disaster. We're all waiting for the next disaster. But the Lord tells us to dwell on what is true, honorable, pure, and lovely, and things that are excellent and commendable. Those who control our media are not content to report the news. They want to create and decide the news. They would much prefer that you act as well-behaved, caged gerbils, spinning in your little metal wheels, stopping only to be breathlessly spellbound by the latest disaster or heinous deed committed by some dark soul. In the mass media as well as Hollywood, and now social media, eyeballs are money – selling your eyeballs on their ad space is their business. But, they want to train you to become obedient little eyeballs. Buried within every storyline is a political agenda they hope will shape your thoughts, your vote, and your life.

The Alpha Male doesn't make for a good media trainee. The Alpha Male's discernment and wisdom, led by the Holy Spirit, doesn't make for a good gerbil. The media's impatience with your obstinacy becomes irritation followed by fear and hatred. If you've ever wondered why it seems that so many in the government and media don't seem to like Christians, this is the reason. The founders of this nation warned us that gerbils could not maintain what they built and gave to us to protect. We stand at that precipice as a nation, but the real loss is not political but spiritual. The fear and hate churned up by the media for all things spiritual – particularly Christianity – gushes into the population. It is a drumbeat that sours them to God's appeal to their souls. Numbed young men put their heads down and try to get by – make a living, drive a cool car, and stay out of trouble with the law. Try to find a girlfriend at the bar on weekends.

The number of people in this country is growing that have no idea who Jesus is, or why what He did is the most important fact on the planet. Numbness is setting in, and along with it is an empty hopelessness that has suicide numbers increasing at an alarming rate, especially among the young. Christians are portrayed in all aspects of media as mean and small-minded bigots who are judgmental, cruel, and need to be controlled by the government so that they're not able to offend anyone. Pretty quickly it could start looking like the Church of England. There is a strong temptation for "good-hearted people" to follow this self-advertised benevolent and praise-worthy government leadership because it claims to be so kind and fair.

The scaffolding of social order, justice and charity that exists in modern society was the result of The Church – The Bride of Christ. Without the Bride, the descent into lawlessness is guaranteed by the ugly heart of unrepentant Man. The promise of Communism is unity *without* God. People will tell you, "Oh, Socialism is different – it's not Communism." Communism is the steel hand inside the velvet glove of Socialism. Josef Stalin, the murderous madman who ran the Soviet Union for so many years of awful destruction of life, warned us that *"The goal of Socialism is Communism."* He wasn't kidding. You can believe that's exactly what he meant, and nothing has changed, regardless of any new packaging you might see. But, the media and many politicians will rush to tell you that the resistance against this vital solution to all of our problems is all scare tactics. These tactics are meant to drive you away from man's ultimate destination – divine glory and unity without having to involve God, or having to acknowledge that He's even there. The great Catholic historian Hillaire Belloc notes in his book The Great Heresies:

> *"...Communism is full slavery...the modern enemy working openly. (It) denies God, denies the dignity and therefore the freedom of the human soul, and openly enslaves men to what it calls "The State" – but what is in practice a body of favored officials. Under full Communism there would be no unemployment, just as there is no unemployment in a prison."*

Man looks longingly at Unity – a touchstone of life – a treasured goal of eternal peace and order. Communism says you can have that treasured Unity, without God. It tells you that there is no such thing as sin, and no need for repentance. Everything is relative. There is not a judgment day coming. Right now you can *be* God, all by yourself, but with their help, of course. The echo of that claim is like a thunderclap, resounding across the vast reaches of time before time began:

> *You said in your heart, "I will ascend to the heavens; I will raise my throne above the stars of God; I will sit enthroned on the mount of assembly, on the utmost heights of Mount Zaphon. I will ascend above the tops of the clouds; I will make myself like the Most High" (Isaiah 14:13-14).*

That hasn't worked out well for Satan – the Accuser – and it won't work out well, ever, for anyone. Make no mistake, God's plan *is* Unity

– the Bride of Christ (that's us) unified with Christ, himself. The Alpha Male longs for that unity, but he knows that the only path to it is the real one laid out before the foundations of creation – in Yeshua, the Christ. The Alpha Male is animated and energized by that call of God and works toward that day when the Son will return for His Bride.

One of the strong traits that the Lord has placed within woman is her capacity for empathy. But, darkness has invaded and intruded upon that trait, and her empathy is being hijacked to rush to the aid of situations and people who don't need or deserve either her empathy or her energy – at least not in the way that they want it. Meanwhile, there is a continuous invention of new victims that must be nurtured and protected, and she will be called on again and again to fight to protect them. If Communism comes to America it will be through the destruction of the Alpha Male and the stolen empathy of women as they make confused choices about what their empathy should feed and empower. A towering need in our culture is the realignment of women's empathy, prying it away from the claws of imaginary social justice and back to the purposes of God.

Christianity is Not a faction

But, in the midst of all this political posturing and earthly kingdom building, Christianity is not a political party or a faction. It is a relationship founded in the sacrifice Jesus made on the cross that made possible the complete forgiveness of the sins of God's most important creation – mankind with free will. There is strong peer pressure within the Christian community to have a certain political bent or persuasion. Much of it has been redirected to these political social justice "issues." Most Christians are strongly anti-abortion. But, we actually have a community of "believers" in Christianity that will tell you that abortion is fine if it's used "properly" and is an expression of women's "rights and advancement" to their true place of authority in our society. Not only that – evil can be good if used for the right end result.

"Woe to those who call evil good and good evil..." (Isaiah 5:20).

It's very hard to imagine how this kind of thinking has become acceptable in any part of the Body of Christ. We even have politicians telling us that it's okay to kill the baby if you do it right away after they're born, but you can't kill them a month later – at least, not yet – not until we can come up with a really good argument. Hanging out in the middle ground is a vast sea of Christians. They are either so caught up in life they don't have time to consider what they're up against, or they've been scattered by the incessant hammering of the media against Christians. They just want to stick their heads in the sand to see if they can make it all go away.

"I know your deeds, that you are neither cold nor hot. I wish you were either one or the other! So, because you are lukewarm—neither hot nor cold—I am about to spit you out of my mouth" (Revelation 3:16).

The truth is not in the middle, in some grand compromise between death and life. The truth is with God and He's glad to share it with you every day. There is a storm brewing. There is an end is coming. I can't tell you how soon, but the signs are becoming more frequent and more significant. The attacks against Christianity are increasing around the globe, not just in America. In fact, by comparison, we have it much better as Christians in the U.S. than in most other countries. In the meantime, don't be deceived. While your attention needs to be on Kingdom matters, as a citizen of this earth you have an earthly responsibility to be informed and to cast your vote, while you still have one. Recall that activist judges with a political persuasion were able to dig through the Constitution and find a long-hidden right for women to kill their babies. Fifty million+ dead babies later, babies are still dying as a statement of a "right to privacy." This from a government that now routinely invades your privacy in unimaginable ways. But, your vote is not the destination or purpose of the Church. It is simply performing a duty that you have as a citizen. Beyond that, your efforts are fragmented and weakened when you allow the politically generated chaos of the day to dictate your Kingdom assignments, and where your energy and focus go. Your time is too precious to waste on every little thing the enemy of your soul is doing. When you engage the enemy in the political realm, focus on the big ones. Remember that he has no power unless you agree with him. So, you know what to do – don't ever agree with him.

Parents and grandparents need to be much more diligent to involve their young ones in the life of the Spirit. Children are very open to spiritual matters – they haven't been jaded and worn down yet by the world. They haven't had a real chance, yet, to foul themselves with the stench of the world. They are much more ready to receive and they're going to need to take their spiritual lives to the next level – beyond anything like what you and I have experienced. The books of Daniel and Revelation tell a stunning tale of what will happen someday and those that are here to see it will need preparation and wisdom that we can only barely imagine, to withstand it and prevail. This is not a call to start building bunkers and storing food. This is a call to hear God's voice and respond. Start now.

Binding the Strong Man

In Hebrew the letters Aleph and Bet, the first two letters of their alphabet, combine to give the word "Av," or "Ab" (rhymes with Bob) meaning "father." Digging back into the original pictographic Hebrew lettering, we find that the symbols used to represent the word "father" are the combination of the symbol Aleph, meaning "ox" or "strength," and the Bet giving the meaning "tent" or "home." The resulting combination of these characters gives the meaning "strength of the home," or "father" – Av, the Alpha Male.

The pictographic characters for mother are Aleph and Mem for the word "em" (rhymes with team), or "ema." Aleph still represents "strong," and Mem represents "water," giving the meaning "strong water" – which translates to glue. In ancient times, boiling animal skins in water produces glue – strong water. The mother, then, is the glue or bond that holds the family together. If the father is the strength of the house then suddenly what Jesus stated about taking over the strong man's house makes a lot of sense.

> *"In fact, no one can enter a strong man's house without first tying him up. Then he can plunder the strong man's house" (Mark 3:27).*

If you can tie up the father of the house or take away his strength, then plundering his house is suddenly very easy. Binding the strong man of the house is exactly what dark forces, using all aspects of education, the media, and government, are trying to do to American men. They would prefer to bind the man *before* he becomes the strong man. A young man raised up with no knowledge of the Alpha Male and his role in this world is much easier to tie up and defeat. If you destroy the strength of the husband and father, the house is no longer defended and you can have your way with the house and the wife and children in it. That's the plan. Don't go along with it.

The Lord is the Ultimate Alpha Male. He created us in His image – His "demuth" (in Hebrew, sounds like demooth) – an exact likeness in kind. He wants to see us express His attributes, willingly and gratefully, in our lives. He loves to see it. He wants to see you be the Alpha Male – it's who He created you to be. The expression of His traits in us is a declaration of Glory and Honor directed towards Him. So, what does He love and what would He like to see in us?

The Lord would like to see you:

1) Love Him with all your heart (Mark 12:33)
2) Love your neighbor as yourself (Leviticus 19:18)
3) Humble yourself (2 Chronicles 7:14)
4) Persevere under trials (James 1:12)
5) Quick to listen (James 1:19)
6) Slow to speak (James 1:19)
7) Slow to become angry (James 1:19)
8) Do what the Word says (James 1:22)
9) Look after orphans and widows (James 1:27)
10) Not show favoritism (James 2:1)
11) Demonstrate the fruit of the Spirit by being loving, joyful, forbearing, kind, good, faithful, gentle and self-controlled (Galatians 5:22-23)

This is a pretty good, if incomplete, description and certainly gives us strong direction in which to direct our energies.

Chapter 10 – Unoffendable

"Write injuries in dust, benefits in marble." - Benjamin Franklin

Offense and Love

Doing unto others and loving like Jesus means giving up being offended, and the badge-of-righteous-suffering that demonstrates how spiritual we are. On an almost humorous note, giving up being offended means *actual* suffering until you get good at giving it up. The longer you are offended, the more you will suffer. So, get good at giving up being offended, pretty quickly. To let go of offense is to give God an opportunity to use you as a collaborator in His plans, rather than to act as a stumbling block for those around you. Life is a full contact sport. As a culture, we've gone from the "Red Badge of Courage" to the "Yellow Badge of Self-Righteous Indignation." The new culture proudly displays its bright yellow t-shirts emblazoned with "I've Been Offended – Do Not Try To Comfort Me While I'm 'In the Moment.'" The trap of righteous indignation is perpetual victimhood. God's children are NOT victims – *"we are more than conquerors through Him who loved us"* (Romans 8:37).

John H. Ingle

Entitlement Produces Victims

You are not entitled to good service. You are not entitled to good products. You may enjoy them and appreciate them, but it is not an entitlement. You are not entitled to perfection and a complete absence of inconvenience in your life. Entitlement is the demand that you be treated differently than everyone else because of who you are – or, at least, who you might *think* you are. The sense of entitlement sets us up for disappointment – disappointment in our fellow man and in God for making us "suffer" at the hands of all these fools and sorry people who just can't seem to get it together. Every moment that sets up as a possible disappointment is a kingdom moment waiting to be birthed. We can be offended and suffer "wrong" and pout or we can look for God's moment there – opening up a miracle pathway between Heaven and Earth – reaching into someone's life to see the promise there, and point them to it. When you point them to it and demonstrate God's love and power, their eyes can be opened and then they can see. What they will see is love and truth, and the uncorking of that desire to hear and know more.

Entitlement is woven strongly throughout Socialism and the Nanny State. Your prior wounding – your affliction – your bad hair day – is justification for all sorts of bad behavior, because you were offended! That offense is then intended to become a "Get out of Jail Free" card that entitles you to become exempt from responsibility, and dependent upon others to feed you, clothe you, care for you, and give you rights even God didn't know you had. It also entitles you to be moody and snooty. Gratefulness, Mercy, Love and Grace are the antidotes to the bondage of entitlement. The Civil Rights Movement of the 1960s began with those attributes and ended a couple of decades later with anger, hate, entitlement, and jealousy. Much of that was caused by the movement being pushed into victimhood – not by the Civil Rights leaders that led the way, but by the professional hucksters and partisans who joined in when they saw the opportunity to make a lot of money off of the whole movement for decades to come. Dr. Martin Luther King preached *"I have a dream,"* but it has been a hollow echo in the Civil Rights movement since not long after his death. Entitlement of every stripe is Big Business in the halls of government. Being a victim is bondage. It enslaves one to the position of location, rather than identity. That bondage can prevent you from moving or escaping victim status because of the fear of the loss of entitlement claims that went with it. Entitlement – the never-ending payday – is the endgame of victimhood, and it's a blind alley.

The Offense

When confronted with someone's claim of offense, the defensive weapon in the believer's hand will be to ask of the Lord, "What is their need?" The alternative is to become equally offended in return, which leads only to anger, and the loss of love. Offense brings judgment. Judgment leads us to attempt to scale the throne to sit in the Holy Seat of God. Sometimes, an offense can be so disturbing and unsettling that walking around it may be your only choice. Understanding everything is not a requirement in our spiritual lives on this planet. There are too many things that we will never understand in this lifetime.

Jesus told his disciples:

> *"...unless you eat the flesh of the Son of Man and drink his blood, you have no life in you" (John 6:53).*

His disciples were shocked, perplexed and casting about for some kind of understanding, but couldn't find any. They were dumbfounded. They told him:

"This is a hard teaching. Who can accept it?" (John 6:53)

Hard teaching, indeed. At that moment, many of His disciples turned back and no longer followed Jesus. Jesus turned back to the twelve and asked:

"You do not want to leave too, do you?" (John 6:57).

Simon Peter had no means of dealing with what Jesus was saying. It was beyond him and he was at a loss at what to do. He had to finally give it up, walk around the perceived offense and remove it from between them, saying to Jesus:

"Lord, to whom shall we go? You have the words of eternal life." (John 6:68 NKJV).

Jesus responded by stating that yes, he had chosen *them*. The underlying message is that those who had turned back were not ready to go where He was about to go.

Chapter 11 – Gratefulness

Training the Heart and Tongue

Once we get a grip on the fact that the Commandments and the Law point us to our fallen state and our helplessness in it, we're ready to face the ultimate reality – God's magnificent grace gave us a savior to pull us up from the pit and restore us to the life He had planned for us from the beginning. At that moment we can experience gratefulness – gratefulness that comes from an understanding of just how bad off we were and aren't any more, due to the love of the Father. We now know what gratefulness means. Gratefulness is that welling up of our spirit in realization of great good that has been given to us. Thanksgiving is the outward display of that gratefulness towards a loving Father. Thanksgiving and gratefulness combine to become a pathway into God's presence.

The challenge of a mind that is keenly aware of quality and excellence is the tendency to always see only the faults in something and be dragged down by the continuing awareness of them. I've had many years of an engineering-oriented career, doing all sorts of normally invisible tasks. My job was often to find the source of problems and lead the development of a remedy. I sometimes joked that my employer provided me with a big, red fire truck and a Dalmatian, and

I was off to fight another fire. It was a bit of a struggle not to always look at something through those eyes and then find the problem in just about everything. I can show you how badly chairs are arranged in a restaurant, as well as show you how an improper curing of wiring cable insulation can cause it to shrink through heat cycling as it ages, potentially causing destructive short-circuits. All of this potentially negative outlook in the middle of daily life can be a challenge to know and still be grateful and live in joy. It can undermine the heart of gratefulness and the giving of thanks, leaving one focused on what may not be "perfect" about life at the moment rather than resting in a heart of joy. The cure for it is to insist on returning to thankfulness for what one has and what God is doing in your life.

Don't Compare

Comparing is a sickness – a search for personal justification, victimhood, or superiority. It is sin – toxic. Don't compare people, or their circumstances. Compare cars, compare recipes, and compare paint colors for the living room. When you compare what gifts and talents you received with what someone else received, you are judging God. Don't compare people. To do so brings us to a place of judgment, and that's a bad place to be.

> *"Each one should test their own actions. Then they can take pride in themselves alone, without comparing themselves to someone else, for each one should carry their own load" (Galatians 6:4-5).*

Instead, speak God's truth into peoples' lives – they are sons and daughters of the Most High, cherished by Him, having been given a plan of salvation, deliverance, and restoration by Him. They're not in your way – they *are* your way. God put them in your path to deliver His message. Be a faithful steward of that task that He's given you.

Deliver the message. Rejoice in the awesome place God has placed you and feel the gratefulness and thanksgiving well up from your heart – then you are fully activated to deliver.

> *"...it is out of the abundance of the heart that the mouth speaks" (Luke 6:45b NRSV).*

Drink in the joy and peace that the Father provides and get your heart and tongue calibrated to the overflow that brings glory to the Father of Lights, in whom there is no shadow of turning.

Building Each Other Up

As King Solomon wrote, *"The tongue has the power of life and death" (Proverbs 18:21a).* We can build people up or we can tear them down. Tearing them down is a dangerous matter – Jesus said that *"...anyone who says, 'You fool!'* (which literally means an atheist or morally corrupt) *will be in danger of the fire of hell" (Matthew 5:22).* That fiery statement *"You fool!"* is intended to accuse someone of being a God-hater, or someone who rejects God. In those days in Israel that was about the worst thing you could say to someone. It's clear that Jesus was very serious about the power of the tongue and what it speaks into someone's life.

> *"The tongue also is a fire, a world of evil among the parts of the body...With the tongue we praise our Lord and Father, and with it we curse human beings, who have been made in God's likeness. Out of the same mouth come praise and cursing. My brothers and sisters, this should not be" (James 3:6a, 9 – 10).*

Judging others is a temptation of the tongue, and we all probably already know that judging is God's territory and we venture into it against all the best advice the Bible can give. So, knowing that we can set the world on fire with our tongues, what else can the tongue do? It can bring the power of life. It can bring blessing. It can bring joy. It can bring comfort. It can bring healing. It can bring love. It can bring salvation to one who needs to hear it. What a miraculous thought that our tongue has such awesome power. It's almost too much to contemplate – but it's true. Speaking into the life of another person is a holy and awesome action that needs to be done with great spiritual care. We see the word "exhort" several times in the Bible. Out in the desert we see John the Baptist *exhorting* the people and proclaiming the good news to them. He is encouraging them to action. He is speaking into their lives with the power of life and the strength of hope – the power of God. And, they were responding.

Releasing Heaven

One of the awesome abilities we get to improve on in life is patience. Hardly anyone is looking for more life situations that require us to develop more patience. Patience assumes that you are in a position of giving rather than receiving. Patience is waiting for the person with whom you are interacting to come to a position where they're actually able to receive. You're waiting for them to give up just "wanting." The "want" can be so strong that it drowns out hearing. The Israelites in the wilderness had that problem. They wanted so desperately that even when provision came, they were still preoccupied with complaining about something that wasn't how they wanted it. It's that victim spirit, again – so focused on what it thinks is lacking that it drowns out gratefulness for what is already possessed. The world is in a hurry. It's hard to be patient and in a hurry at the same time. Don't let the world dictate your speed or the amount of time that you are ready to spend, waiting for someone to hear. If God has put them smack dab in your path, and He's given you an assignment there, patience is what He's

The Alpha Male

expecting you to spend on them. It can be a hard thing to do, but it's what they need.

Chapter 12 – Greater Works Than These

"The Cross is where forgiveness was given but the resurrection was where the power was released. We have been taught to receive the forgiveness but we have not been taught to receive and live in the power of the resurrection. The ascension of Jesus to the right hand of the Father is where authority to release the power was obtained. The death - burial - resurrection - and ascension is the full gospel. It takes all four for us to walk in the fullness of salvation." Janice Seney

Walking in the fullness of salvation, by necessity, requires us to deal with a few of the promises that Jesus made to his followers. The first one that I bring to your attention is:

"Very truly, I tell you, the one who believes in me will also do the works that I do and, in fact, will do greater works than these, because I am going to the Father" (John 14:12 NRSV).

Let's look at some of the things Jesus had done so far in His time here. He:

1. Turned water into wine

The Alpha Male

2. Healed the official's son without even going to see him
3. Healed the invalid at the Bethesda pool
4. Fed thousands with the young boy's five barley loaves and two small fish
5. Walked on water out to the boat
6. Commanded the wind and waves to be still and they did it.
7. Healed a man on the Sabbath in the temple.
8. Gave sight to a man that was born blind
9. Raised Lazarus from the dead
10. Forgave sins
11. Too many other things to mention

Was he talking about <u>these things</u> that we would be able to do greater than? Do you believe it? It's not the only time He said something like this. Did He misspeak? A slip of the tongue? You can't pick and choose from what Jesus said to construct your own version of the Bible. Either you believe all of what He said or you don't. My recommendation is that we believe Him. Now, we have to figure out why these things aren't happening. I don't think it's Him. That leaves us.

Why aren't we seeing this type of activity on a regular basis? Well, for starters, we see a whole lot more miracles happening in countries that don't enjoy the same level of creature comforts that we do. They also appear to be much more open to the possibility of miracles than in this country. In Middle Eastern countries, large numbers of Muslims are being saved through dreams. Jesus is appearing to them and they're being converted, even though they know it could mean a death sentence if found out. How's that for a miracle? It's happening – <u>a lot</u>. We are so jaded in Western culture that, as I talked about previously, we want a comfortable, rational explanation – anything but a miracle. We find ourselves so cozy and snuggled into our comfort zones, that to come out is almost like punishment. And, miracles are scary. The limits of our faith are the ones we put there, so as to not scare ourselves.

I'm pretty sure that if you believe that you are not able to be closely involved in miracles in Jesus' name and through the power of God then you probably won't be. The question remains, *"When the son of man returns, will he find faith on the earth?"* How much faith do we dare have? How much do we dare use? I am again reminded of the story of the Ten Talents. If you don't remember that one you might want to go find it and read it, again.

Jesus Promises the Holy Spirit

> *"But the Advocate, the Holy Spirit, whom the Father will send in my name, will teach you all things and will remind you of everything I have said to you" (John 14:26).*

So, wait a minute – the Holy Spirit is going to teach me things? How is He going to do that? It will be through me hearing Him – the voice of God. I will need to listen and do – hear and respond. There are many Christians who would want to condemn me and maybe even throw me out of the Church over this statement – that it is sacrilege – that it's placing me above God, or at least above His Word. It's all about me, now. No. It's not. It's the Uncreated God-Head – the Trinity – telling me this – in His Word.

> *"...the Spirit of truth. The world cannot accept him, because it neither sees him nor knows him" (John 14:17a).*

Those who insist that I can't hear from God and that the Holy Spirit is not going to teach me things have to ponder whether it is because they neither see Him nor know Him that they think that. That should be the thing that shocks them in all of this. It is as if they live in a parallel dimension that cannot see into this one, because, that's exactly what's happening. If you have the Holy Spirit, you already do live in a different dimension. The fact that they can't see it should be what wakes them up. That is where I recommend that the focus remains – on getting to know Him, through His Holy Spirit, which indwells all believers who acknowledge and welcome the presence of the Holy Spirit.

Jesus Sends Out the Seventy-two

Jesus told his disciples that the harvest is huge, but the workers are few. If you are a believer, then you are part of the few. That means there's plenty of work to go around. The good news is that God does the work. We just need to pay attention to what He's doing and join in with Him. That's how He wants it. When the inconveniences of life happen, look around and see what He's doing there. It is very possible that He has made a divine appointment for you. And, you don't have to guarantee the outcome. He does. And, in doing what He sets before you it will increase your faith and your faithfulness. One of His children needs a word, perhaps. If so, He will give it to you at the right moment. Maybe they need a healing. It is in your calling to pray for their healing.

> *"Heal the sick who are there and tell them, 'The kingdom of God has come near to you'" (Luke 10:9).*

The word "near" in that verse is not very well represented with the Greek rendering. In Hebrew, the language being used by Jesus and the apostles, the word "near" has a connotation of a lot more than somewhere close by. After all, in Isaiah 8:3 we see that the prophet Isaiah "came near the prophetess (his wife), and she conceived and bore a son" (Bivin, Blizzard). So, Heaven is a lot closer than "near" you. The invitation and the guidance are clearly to inhabit Heaven – The Kingdom – now, from where you are.

Your Spirit is Your Plumage

If you've never seen a male peacock in its dance routine as it throws its plumage into a big fan of shimmering colors and "eyes," you should run out to the internet and find a good video of one. It is really impressive. Likewise, the male redbird is striking in the richness of its color. The male lion's mane is just an introduction to his strength and authority. But, the world, for all its natural riches and wonders, can be a pretty grimy place.

> *"Whoever walks in the dark does not know where they are going" (John 12:35c).*

Jesus also said:

> *"I am the light of the world. Whoever follows me will never walk in darkness, but will have the light of life" (John 8:12).*

If you have the light of life, and are supposed to be salt and light to the world, then that means that <u>*you don't look like the world*</u>. It will, or should be, quickly obvious to most people that there is something different about you…that you don't look like everyone else. What is it?

Think back, again to the male cardinal with its bright red color, and the male peacock with its amazing fan plumage. What do *you* have? You have the Holy Spirit, if you've asked. Through the Holy Spirit you have salt (for flavor) and light (for guidance and illumination).

The Alpha Male

Your plumage is your spirit. It either provides salt and light or it does not. Jesus prefers that it does both, which is why he said:

> *"You are the salt of the earth...You are the light of the world. A town built on a hill cannot be hidden. Neither do people light a lamp and put it under a bowl. Instead they put it on its stand, and it gives light to everyone in the house. In the same way, let your light shine before others, that they may see your good deeds and glorify your Father in heaven" (Matthew 5:13a, 14 -16).*

According to Jeff Benner at the Ancient Hebrew Research Center, Hebrew "is a concrete oriented language meaning that the meaning of Hebrew words are rooted in something that can be sensed by the five senses such as a tree which can be seen, sweet which can be tasted, and noise which can be heard."

He also maintains, as many Hebrew scholars do, that abstract concepts have no foundation in Hebrew and are a product of ancient Greek philosophy. A Greek translation or transliteration of Hebrew necessarily stuffs in all sorts of Greek ways of thinking as part of the process. It also makes a lot of assumptions that don't stand up under close scrutiny. Greek is very linear and has a tendency to steamroll over Hebrew nuance and idiom, modifying the original meaning. It is as if two hundred years from now someone finds a note I left saying, "See you later, alligator!" After much study, linguists would issue the following translation: "I will see you in some future time in the afternoon or evening, large reptile." It just doesn't have the same flavor, don't you agree?

Jesus is speaking of salt and light in a very Jewish way, using the Hebrew language in its fullest essence. Light exposes things, ideas, and intent. The light God wants to see is His love, alive through you and being exposed to all of His creation. Your light shining before others has a very important function – it is your plumage – not for your ego, not for your personal enjoyment, but as a sign for the salvation of the nations.

Who you attract is a reflection of what your spirit is projecting. Bill Johnson of Bethel Church says that, *"Our countenance will release the reality of the world we are most aware of."* Countenance is a complex word, meaning a summation of many components – our facial expressions and demeanor, our emotional stability, even our life-vision. It's a view into our spirit. It all shows in our countenance. If our countenance is releasing a grim awareness of the defeats and endless perils of life, many will withdraw from embracing that vision or seeking its counsel.

However, if our countenance is releasing a radiance that reflects the God we serve and love, then we become attractive to many and they will come closer to find out what you have that creates this warmth that draws them in. This overall attraction is a sign of significant importance to the female because it also reflects the warmth and safety she seeks for nourishing and protecting the family. It verifies that you are a man of God, reflecting His glory. You could try to fake it, but then your countenance would show the world fakery and deception. People will see that, whether they tell you or not. It has to be real.

The fact that women are strongly attracted to this plumage of the Spirit-filled Alpha Male, explains how men of God can be tempted to enter into illicit love relationships within the Church, particularly among its pastoral staff. Women who are not joined with an Alpha Male can be drawn, without realizing why, towards that Spirit-filled man, especially when they spend considerable time together as staff members. It is something for which she is actively searching if she hasn't found it yet. It is not even necessary that the woman be spiritually aware or mature – she can be drawn, anyway. It is an absolute requirement to have firm rules in place for yourself and those around you so that your plumage is not diminished by erecting barriers around yourself, but you also don't fall into temptation and stain you and your Church Body. King David can give you more detailed information on that topic.

Your Territory

The Alpha Male has a territory. That territory is not to own as if it were a piece of property. It is a territory in which the Lord is giving you a gift or an anointing that He wants you to release into that territory. There will be obstacles that attempt to present themselves. Powers will move against your ownership – especially those powers that are being displaced. You may see Christians, or those claiming to be, being recruited by and siding with these opposing powers. These are people who are not firm in their faith, but are weak in their faith, being manipulated and *"blown about by every wind of doctrine."* BUT, they are not the enemy. As always, we're not warring against flesh and blood.

Territories overlap in both the physical and spiritual worlds. What God has given you to release is not the same as what He has given to another, and there is not a competition in this arena. Your spirit is aware of spiritual activity going on around you. Your spirit's awareness can go before you when you enter a room, or a new environment. The Holy Spirit, within, will "see" the other spirits in the room, whether they bring good or evil. A fully developed Alpha Male will begin to pray and speak to the room before he even sees who is in it, and what they're doing there.

John H. Ingle

Healing – Body and Mind

So many times in my lifetime I've heard people say that God gave them this disease, or that disaster, or this loss of a loved one, cancer, broken bones, job loss, and so on. It usually comes down to the claim that God is punishing them for something they did wrong, or is using a proactive punishment on them to force them to be more holy and more obedient. I don't know what to make of that except that it doesn't sound like the God I serve. I'm brought back again to what God showed me about the stones falling from the sky as Joshua's army took up a position to watch – the stones were already on the way – Joshua just needed to know where to stand, and the Lord gave him direction. But, all too often we're not able to hear His voice or see what He's doing, because we're so caught up in something else that He's being drowned out of our life for a moment or for a decade. At that point, God is not the one who gave me grief or heartache because of something I did – I may have given myself that heartache – I may have even worked hard to earn it. I certainly earned all the heartbreak of my first marriage. The Lord told me not to do it. I had a better plan…I thought. And, yes, I did go back to her some years later and apologize for refusing God's counsel and going against His best advice. The fact was that the marriage should never have happened and would not have if I had been behaving as the Alpha Male. But, consequences are not the same thing as punishment. The Lord didn't *punish* me for that marriage, but I earned all the sad consequences of it. If my mind wanders while I'm pounding in framing nails and I smash my thumb, it's not a punishment from God – it's a consequence of not paying attention.

The God I serve can certainly take lemons and make lemonade. He can take the bad things of life and bless them and make them serve a purpose for His Kingdom. He can use the wisdom we gained from a

The Alpha Male

consequence to bless His Kingdom. That's where our hope is – in the expectation of good – of blessing. In Hebrew, the whole concept of hope is tied to the Redeemer, the Savior – He is hope, personified. Without Him, there is no hope.

When my real wife, Esta (the one He was saving for me), was diagnosed with breast cancer I was on a business trip in the northeast. She called to tell me what the doctor had told her. Without thinking about it even for a moment I began to prophesy aloud to her – to speak into her life and to her spirit. However, the words didn't come from me. They came from the Holy Spirit. I told her that the Lord would bring healing and that she would become a sharp knife in His hand for His kingdom, as He uses her for good rather than to suffer evil.

A short time later He explained that she would become a sharp knife in cutting through ropes of bondage in the Church body. He did, and she was, and still is. I had believed it and so did she. When those in the church body began to gather around her saying, "Poor Esta," God spoke to her through me again, "No, not poor Esta…RICH Esta…rich in my blessings, rich in my spirit, rich in the healing and mercy I provide. Don't drink from this cup of sadness…there is despair and pain in that cup, not comfort and life." He didn't want her to become a victim; He wanted her to become a victor. "Poor Esta" would not be a victor, but "RICH Esta" certainly would be, and is.

Chapter 13 – Fearfully and Wonderfully Made

Our bodies are a crazy electro-chemical stew, with chemicals, molecules and cells along with their receptor sites and ion channels constantly churning and moving – a sort of Rube Goldberg Machine where the ball goes down the ramp, spins the wheel, which turns a paddle, that winds a spring mechanism, dropping the ball into a different chamber where it jumps over into some other domino action, and speeds merrily along. The human body contains a staggering amount of activities and motions all happening at the same time at any one moment, sort of like a multitude of those machines all playing off of each other in three or four dimensions.

At the cellular level we have agonists, superagonists, antagonists, receptors and their biological responses or non-responses operating on a continuous basis. These chemicals and activities can decide whether we're asleep or awake, sedated or chatting merrily with friends, or experiencing pain, and so forth. If a virus (little miniature terrorist) is trying to gain entry to a cell it will first try to bind to a cell surface receptor, cozying up to the cell membrane to get entry. Then, it will work to convince the cell to take it in as if it were some sort of nourishment. Once inside, pandemonium breaks loose. It hijacks the cell's replication mechanism, slams in its own blueprint software and instructs the cell to "make more of me." All of this can be going on while you're having coffee with coworkers in the cafeteria. You don't have to be personally involved to soon become personally involved. Suddenly, the intruder is detected and your entire immune system is running up red flags and sounding alarms, again without your direct involvement, and often with little awareness of the war that's about to happen. You're just feeling a little rundown and you've sneezed a couple of times.

Infectious organisms, along with what we eat, breathe, drink or consume in any fashion, can become a part of that wildly complex machine's operation for a period of time, sometimes, potentially for the remainder of a lifetime. I saw a study quite a few years back regarding lead levels in the soil near freeways of old northeastern inner cities. Lead tetraethyl used to be added to gasoline to improve its performance. Daily traffic released these toxic lead compounds into the air, whereupon they settled into the soil around those freeways. The areas where these toxic lead compounds settled were largely poor neighborhoods, and the absorption of these compounds through the skin caused brain damage in a lot of the local children over time. They didn't have to eat or drink anything as they played in their yards, and they and their parents had no idea what was happening to them. Those toxic lead levels altered the nervous systems of many children before the cause was discovered. Those alterations were life-changing for those children and their families, and not in a good way.

There is an old saying that "We are what we eat." To a degree there is truth in that statement, in that we are adding ingredients into a constantly moving system that may determine whether we'll be tired, irritable, relaxed, nervous, happy, sad, depressed, or whatever, and for how long. It's an amazing system. Despite the enormous complexity of the human body, there are those that argue that it just kinda happened by accident over the eons, and now, here you are, no longer seaweed. The Lord was not kidding when He told us that we are "fearfully and wonderfully made." You're not a freak cosmic accident, acting as the little steel ball in some galaxy-wide pinball game.

Your body has a chemical profile. Our habits, our diet and our emotions all add to and modify that profile, sometimes to the point of appearing permanent. The semi-permanent distortion of that profile can take a toll on our self-image, as we struggle to apprehend God's great love for us. How can He? Why would He? The feelings of unworthiness can become so profound and so overwhelming that we are tempted to feel justification in our suffering. We deserve it, and make it a partner in life. Our spouse and children just need to learn that sad fact and submit to a life of sorrow and pain just as we have. Many abused children grow up with a certain knowledge that they are unlovable, and most seem to believe that it is justifiably so.

Our spirit and our physical body are intertwined, with one affecting the other in somewhat predictable ways, but also in other, unknown ways. We know that if we eat plenty of food loaded with unhealthy fats, and get no exercise, our relationship with a Cardiologist will likely become much closer, and our life expectancy, shorter. We know that if we drink something with a lot of caffeine in it, we may experience symptoms that remind us that we did that. If you ingest an alcoholic beverage, your reaction times are going to slow and your spatial orientation may suffer. At the same time, our minds contribute to that activity and motion that's going on in our body. When we are emotionally distressed, it shows up in chemical activities that spread throughout the body. But, things can get stuck in a mode that prevents or slows down our ability to control our mood. Mental depression can begin to control the body, as it modifies the chemical activities and their impact on the body, magnifying some activities and suppressing others. Lethargy, lack of energy or motivation, and withdrawing from social activities can all become part of our spiritual/emotional state due to a lack of normal chemical equilibrium in the body. It can stay stuck for a long time, if untended.

Stress, Hormones and Chemicals

Cortisol is known as the stress hormone. It is produced in the adrenal gland and is usually associated in many people's minds with flight-or-fight along with adrenaline. Adrenaline works more in the short term while cortisol is more long term. There are other differences between the two as well, but cortisol is the one that can really bite. It has been called Public Health Enemy #1 by many professionals in medicine and psychology. Cortisol can be a wrecking ball, affecting numerous hormone levels all over the body. Cortisol increases glucose levels in the blood and also raises blood pressure for that fight-or-flight need. Chronically high cortisol levels can even lead to diabetes and osteoporosis. Drinking beverages with caffeine can spike cortisol levels. High cortisol levels can lead to weight gain. An unhealthy level of cortisol is not the only thing that can go wrong in your body regarding the effects of stress.

Under stress, things in the body/brain functionality can literally get rewired. When I say rewired, I mean that there are responses that can become knee-jerk and self-perpetuating. Repetition can form new nervous system pathways, and pathway groups get wired together. In his outstanding book, *"The Body Keeps the Score,"* Dr. Bessel Van Der Kolk notes that "things that wire together fire together" (p. 56). That means that a repetitive sequence can begin to trigger other behaviors that didn't exist before. Van Der Kolk's book is a noteworthy compendium of PTSD history, research and treatments. He is a leading scientific researcher and author in that field.

John H. Ingle

There was a time in my life of overwhelming family tragedy. I lost Joshua – my young adult son from my first marriage. He had gone to the University of Texas as an honor student, where he discovered LSD. He thought it would be good to take it every day. He equated "tripping" with spirituality. Even though we were very close he couldn't hear me imploring him to get away from it. He never recovered from the damage it had done to his mind and he eventually took his own life. It was a very rough time for me and the stress levels rarely receded for long. I cried in the shower every morning for a year. I began to notice subtle changes in my body chemistry that didn't go away. I didn't understand them, but I knew they were happening. When momentary emotional challenges would come up, I noticed that my body had a specific physical reaction that would accompany the emotional reaction, and the reaction was always stronger than in normal times. I could feel my body chemistry change, accompanied by a feeling of almost tunnel vision, with shadows around the edges of my vision when those moments came and went. It literally felt like someone was throwing a switch in my body. I knew it was a chemical change and it seemed to come with its own depression mechanism that amplified whatever immediate emotions were being stirred. And, so began a downward spiral, with one feeding the other. The emotional response would kick off the chemical response, and the chemical response would feed back into the emotional response, with progressively more negative results. It was serious and I had to find ways of dealing with it.

I limped along, knowing that I probably wasn't being a very good husband, or father to my other three sons, either. I saw my blood lab numbers going in the wrong direction and my body succumbing to the ravages of depression. I realized that I had to purposefully look for ways to reduce my stress level and get a handle on things. I had to change my chemistry back to normal. I begged the Lord for help. He responded by giving me a job change where I worked. I was interviewed for a new position at work and suddenly found myself in a well-sheltered environment where I was only asked to do the things I was really good at, and I had executive oversight that let me do pretty much whatever I needed to do to get the job done. The people I worked with were sharp, fun, and a pleasure to work with. My boss didn't act like a boss, but like a friendly mentor. Gradually, the steam began to let off and I found myself responding in more positive ways to stressful events in life. I attended marriage counseling with my wife to learn better ways of communicating. We went through the Peacemakers class with Bob Cave and his late wife Robbie at Central Baptist Church in Round Rock, Texas. Over the course of the next year or so, my wife and I also had additional private counseling sessions with Bob and Robbie, as well. Robbie and I became good friends, and she had a lot to do with pulling me back into the organized body of the Church. Robbie explained to me that men have isolated compartments for everything – nothing touches anything else. Women have one compartment – everything touches everything, like a bowl of spaghetti. That mental picture helped me to better understand the emotions of women. For a woman, when something is wrong, somewhere, it can show up everywhere. Men are just the opposite. They can have a crumbling personal life and no one at work know anything was wrong. I learned a lot about how I had been peace-faking and peace-breaking, rather than peace-making. Robbie began slowly bringing me back into the camp. She worked as a lifeguard for Jesus.

I began to reorient my focus in life away from so much concern about job and career. I began to remind myself daily that I don't work for man, I work for the Lord. I asked a good friend, and former co-worker, to call me up randomly and ask me, "Who do you work for, today?"

Surprisingly, all too often I still would have to answer, "Oh...yeah... that's right – *not* man." Work still had its demands and its numbers and it was still a contest to remember that I really did work for the Lord, and not in order to please men. Slowly I was climbing back out of the downward spiral that would take me mentally and physically down for days at a time. I was healing. Stress is serious stuff.

PTSD – The 900 Pound Gorilla

Our emotional state acts as a filter to the world around us and even to the voice of the Holy Spirit. War after war has produced generations of young men who return to their homes with emotional states that barely allow them a stable physical existence. For many, that emotional filter invites drugs and alcohol in a fruitless attempt to kill the pain and the memories. Nightmares interrupt the sleep patterns and the body suffers from the loss of restorative sleep patterns. Post-Traumatic Stress Disorder (PTSD) is a scourge on the land. Over 30% of Vietnam Veterans have suffered from PTSD. Over 80% of Vietnam Veterans who have been diagnosed with PTSD still suffer from the symptoms today. In 2013, more than 12,000 Iraq and Afghanistan Veterans were diagnosed with PTSD. Likely many thousands more don't even report their symptoms because they don't think they can be helped. Aside from war, PTSD origins also include physical or sexual assault, violent crime, death of a loved one, accidents, or natural disaster – some sort of severe trauma. Dr. Van Der Kolk estimates that there are 10 to 1 more traumatized children than traumatized vets. Most of those traumatized children are victims of sexual assault. That would make for a staggering number of suffering people that need a lot of emotional help and healing. The most common treatment for PTSD is drugs. But, drugs can be a problem for a lot of different reasons, not the least of which concerns the opportunity for normal sexual relations within a marriage.

> *"Sexual dysfunction is a common side effect of antidepressants and can have significant impact on the person's quality of life, relationships, mental health, and recovery."* (Abstract: Antidepressant-associated sexual dysfunction: impact, effects, and treatment)

In that situation, it all too often becomes, "You can get along better with your wife, but you can't have sex with her." Other complications of antidepressants include dry mouth, urinary retention, blurred vision, constipation, sedation (can interfere with driving or operating machinery), sleep disruption, weight gain, headache, nausea, gastrointestinal disturbance/ diarrhea, abdominal pain, loss of libido, agitation, and anxiety (*Side Effects of Antidepressants*, Tyrrell, Elliott). Stopping the drugs typically results in a relapse of the same symptoms. Many PTSD sufferers won't take them or can't take them. The good news is that there are other non-invasive, non-drug treatments being developed and used that are taking the place of drug treatments and hold promise for real help. Way too much emphasis has been placed on drugs rather than other therapies that have lasting results even after the treatments are discontinued.

EMDR and Other Strange PTSD Treatments

Eye Movement Desensitization and Reprocessing (EMDR) is something that lies at the edge of our rational minds when looking at PTSD treatments. When something works and we don't quite fully understand it, it may really just mean that we don't understand it, yet. History is filled with herbal medicines and treatments that were successfully used with absolutely no understanding of why they worked. A perfect example is aspirin – acetylsalicylic acid. Willow tree bark contains salicylic acid, a precursor to what was later synthesized and became known as aspirin. Willow bark tea has been used for almost a couple of thousand years to treat fevers and pain. No one knew why willow tree bark tea made people feel better, but they used it anyway because it worked. In similar fashion, EMDR can be just as odd a treatment as you've ever seen. In addition, it works often enough to make it a real contender in treatment programs. Dr. Van Der Kolk notes that it may be related to Rapid Eye Movement (REM) and offer some of the same type of benefit. He describes its activity as repackaging trauma as a complete memory that can be processed and dealt with, rather than the jagged little pieces of shrapnel that each bring their own pain.

There are other similar, offshoot treatments that are beginning to take hold as well, including hand tapping which may work on the same principle but with a different activator. EMDR is somewhat controversial, but just as willow tree bark gave people relief from fever and pain, EMDR has relieved symptoms of PTSD permanently for many who have tried it.

Another non-invasive, non-drug treatment is Transcranial Magnetic Stimulation (TMS). TMS uses electromagnetic fields to stimulate parts of the brain that are underperforming. The fields act to stimulate neurons, exciting them into activity. Also overlooked is neurofeedback, a very promising treatment that results in permanent improvement, rather than temporary chemical behavior modification. However, all too often, treatments are offered or decided based on what insurance will cover rather than what is effective for the patient.

Sozo

Sozo is a counseling treatment that is gaining traction in Christian circles. I have to admit I didn't like the name for a while. Goombah is an equally good name and it's likely no one else is using it. But, that's what it's called, so we'll go with that. Sozo actually comes from the Greek language, meaning "saved," or "delivered." If you are dealing with trauma, PTSD, recurring guilt feelings, depression, or other persistent off-balance thinking in your life, I strongly recommend that you ask around area churches for someone who is doing Sozo sessions and sign up. I have personally met many people who attest to its effectiveness.

CBD Oil

Cannabidiol oil (CBD) is one of the carbon alkaloids known as cannabinoids that are found uniquely in cannabis sativa (marijuana). These cannabinoids do not contain the psychoactive properties of tetrahydrocannabinol (THC), which is credited with the properties that induce a "high" or intoxication. CBD oil is usually a blend of the extracted cannabinoid with an oil, such as coconut, hemp seed, or olive oil. Many serious studies are documenting the anti-inflammatory properties of CBD oil, and many more are in progress for studying the effectiveness of it against PTSD. It has been suggested that the anti-inflammatory properties alone are very helpful against PTSD, as inflammation typically accompanies the symptoms of PTSD. Reducing inflammation reduces the overall number of trigger points for PTSD. The political aspects of this treatment being derived from marijuana, along with overall lack of knowledge about what it is, contribute to a general fog around its acceptance. Much more research needs to be done in order to publish treatment schedules, methods and concentrations. Formal studies may be slow in coming as they won't likely be done by major pharmaceutical manufacturers who have drug treatments that compete with CBD.

Chasing Loose Cannons

You can't fix her. No matter how pretty, or sexy, or fun she is, if she has serious traumatic damage, you can't fix her. God can fix her. You can't. She will be like the legendary story from the days when cannons were sticking out the sides of wooden warships. Those cannons were mounted in braces that ran on tracks, and had to be chained down with very large, strong chains. If your cannon came loose from its mount and you were in heavy seas, that cannon, which weighed quite a lot, would be bouncing and rolling around below deck, an unpredictable, mortal danger to anyone in its path – the loose cannon that could smash you like a bug on the windshield. She *is* that loose cannon. So, if the gorgeous young thing that you're courting is suffering from traumatic events in her past and she hasn't dealt with the damage with God's help, you could find yourself facing something you don't understand and you can't fix. Not only can you not fix it, you often can't even approach it without stirring up a storm that can run off in any direction and cause big damage to you or anyone close by. Chasing loose cannons is a very dangerous sport.

Emotions

> *"Feelings and emotions left unsupervised are a playground for confusion. Adults enjoy their children but would never turn the household over to them. Even so emotions are to be enjoyed, disciplined, guided and never allowed to be in charge."* - Janice Seney

Emotions are not your spirit. Emotions can run you but you don't have to let them do it. If you make spiritual decisions using emotions as your guideline, get ready to make a lot of bad decisions. That includes positive as well as negative emotions. Positive emotions can be the result of mood swing or even just having a good day with no stressors popping up in your life. Assuming a decision is a good one because you're in a good mood is not a good strategy. This book is not a compendium of sources and methods of treatment for PTSD and chronic depression. But, I can tell you that there is help out there and the Lord is still the Healer.

In the arena of physical and mental healing, Christians are sometimes trapped by their personal mental scorecard that indicates what healing they may qualify for or currently deserve, forgetting that God is a loving God and isn't playing a you-do-this and I'll-do-that transaction with us. One of the things you must do is to give God the things you can't carry. He did say something about his burden being light. Yours may not be. If yours is heavy it's also probably starting to show. Repeatedly returning to the source of one's stress in our minds reinforces the emotion and the chemical response that may go with it. If you're in need, start looking for proven non-pharma ways to stop the repetition and get healed. Get rid of the filters that stand between you and hearing God properly.

Peace

Peace isn't a lack of emotion. Emotions have their place and value because God made them part of who we are. But, there are healthy ways to use them and unhealthy ways. Peace is not a stale existence, having neither joy nor sorrow. Peace is the perfect emotion. It is the emotion of the Godhead, the emotion of the Prince of Peace. Peace for you is complete and relaxed confidence in God's supernatural authority over all creation. He invites you to join Him in that perfect state of being. Peace is not to be confused with the depersonalization reaction from trauma – that out-of-body feeling that life seems to be happening to someone else. Peace is perfect, and Jesus says that He gives us His. Get some of His. He wants you to have it.

Chapter 14 – Marriage – The God Unit

> *"Marriage is...in its origin a contract of natural law... It is the parent, and not the child of society; the source of civility and a sort of seminary of the republic."* - Justice Joseph Story

The public act of marriage is a social construct and a public proclamation. You can become married to someone without a guy in a suit asking you who has which ring. You can both be the only two people on an otherwise deserted island and become married. It is a statement made before God, *to* God and an act of lifetime commitment of the will by each of the participants to each other. It is a unification of your wills to become one – unity. It is a very dangerous act if entered into without serious and thoughtful consideration of the consequences of that act. The final action of entering into a marriage is that the two of you climb, naked, into the same skin, and live right up against each other. Within that covering of skin is complete vulnerability. There are no protections against what the other person might do and the consequences of what they might do. Whatever we do, we do to both of us.

> *"Has He not made you and your wife one? You belong to Him, body and spirit. And what does He seek from such a union? Godly*

children. So guard yourselves; be true to the wife of your youth, and stop being unfaithful. For I, the God of Israel, hate divorce!" (Malachi 2:15-16a, VOICE).

In looking at the Hebrew text, the warning appears even more serious and potentially more suspicious of one's motives. Instead of *"be true to the wife of your youth,"* it looks more like the warning, "let none deal treacherously" with the hint of it meaning to pillage in secrecy (qbible.com).

Marriage is much more than filing joint tax returns each April at tax time. The question can certainly be asked whether a marriage that was not done with God's involvement was ever a marriage to begin with. The marriage may have been little more than sexually active roommates with a county-issued license "permitting" them to cohabitate and file a joint tax return. These are all governmental observations and tradition – rendering unto Caesar what is Caesar's. Government can collect taxes and fees based on how many papers you have to file.

Unity and One Another

Marriage is the ultimate unity that can occur on planet Earth with two of God's creation. It is His earthly demonstration of a principle so dear to Him that He has moved heaven and earth to drive home the message. Out in the world, the storm rages. It's where Satan stalks about like a roaring lion, seeking whom he might accuse and devour. And, devour he does, and he will, again. The Lord uses both marriage and the Church Body as protective barriers against that storm. Marriage is the natural state of the Alpha Male. It is natural in the same sense that God created this physical realm as natural, with our bodies carrying our spiritual essence.

The Alpha Male

Marriage has the covering of God – protection beneath his wings, with the husband as Chief Priest and Alpha Male of the family unit. The wife is the nurturing power inside the unit, keeping it bound together, and she is really good at it. The Church body reinforces and mirrors that covenant-oriented thinking that provides protection and covering over the family. Children, raised out in that storm without that protection, are going to be beaten down and trained to shape themselves to fit into that storm and accommodate it – to become *of* the world. There they are trained to accept deviance and sin of every sort as perfectly normal – something to be proud of, even. If they don't have the firm foundation of God's Word and His Kingdom, they will become jaded and ground down instead of withstanding that storm and subduing it.

Unity is important to the Lord in ways we can't even comprehend. Consider how many times "one another" is used in describing the Church of the New Covenant. I have done a detailed count of these occasions throughout the Bible and I find more than fifty-five times the phrase is used. Good examples of this phrase are:

> *"This is what the Lord Almighty said: 'Administer true justice; show mercy and compassion to one another'" (Zechariah 7:9).*

> *"A new command I give you: Love one another. As I have loved you, so you must love one another" (John 13:34).*

Practically all the times the phrase is used, it's used in the sense of how we are to treat each other. These are guideposts of godly living – good advice – given for your spiritual education and the health of your home and heart.

Marriage is exceedingly important to the Lord. We are told that the "Church" is the Bride of Christ. The Alpha Male is an archetype, or pointer, to the role of Jesus in this Creation in which we live. The Alpha Male's Bride is the archetype, or pointer, to the Bride of Christ – the Church. The Unity of the Alpha Male and his Bride symbolize for us the Unity that The Lord God is planning for Jesus and His Bride – the Church – that Holy Union. What holds true for the one Union is very often true for the other. This wedding on earth – this Unity between a man and a woman – is a magnificent foretelling of the wedding to come. Unity – becoming or being "one" – exists in ways that we cannot even imagine or foretell. It is beyond our ability to comprehend but that does nothing to alter the coming reality of Christ returning for His Bride. Marriages are constantly being attacked, or at least the attempt is made to attack them. The health of many Christians is being attacked. Our jobs are under attack…and our homes. Television and public media continue their downward descent, racing towards the bottom. Many kids' video games routinely present immoral and shockingly bad treatment of our fellow man as a winning strategy…"do unto others before they do unto you." But the Bible quotes Jesus as saying:

> *"… upon this rock I will build my church; and the gates of hell shall not prevail against it" (Matthew 16:18 KJV).*

It says the gates of hell will not be able to stand against the fact that *"Thou art the Christ, the Son of the living God."* Does that sound like we're hunkered down in caves in a defensive mode, afraid to move or venture out? This doesn't describe a retreat; it's an assault against evil.

Unequally Yoked

> *"Do not be unequally yoked together with unbelievers" (2 Corinthians 6:14a, New King James Version).*

The Alpha Male

This verse has been tossed around since shortly after the days of the apostles, but what does it really mean? Consider what it looks like to have two oxen, side-by-side, yoked together, pulling the same plow. One is pulling hard and the other is hardly pulling, or pulling a different direction. They aren't just going slowly, they're moving in a very small circle – they aren't going *anywhere*. Their field won't get plowed that way, and it means there won't be any fruit from all that labor. Your life-mate should not be someone who is pulling against you in your relationship with the Lord and your relationship together absolutely needs to include the Lord. Think of it another way – oil and water don't mix. You can shake them vigorously and they will seem to mix for a few moments, but if you leave the mixture for even a few minutes, it separates back into the two components. They weren't ever "one."

"Sufficient unto the day is the evil thereof" (Matthew 6:34b KJV).

"The day" doesn't need any help from you or your life-mate in creating an even larger dogpile of evil to slosh through. Delilah is the perfect example of a "mate" who was pulling in the wrong direction. Her concern was never for Samson and his well-being. Her concern was for currying favor with someone else based on her ability to bring Samson down. The act of being unequally yoked can be described in a rainbow of colors. It may be the result of past emotional damage that prevents a spouse from seeing the world through God's eyes in a Kingdom-oriented manner. The most famous and perhaps the most common evidence of damage would be "daddy issues," as a result of having an unhealthy or even abusive relationship between daddy and daughter. Or, as is even more common in the present day, there never was a daddy, or he was so distant or disconnected that he almost didn't exist.

Daddy issues can greatly encourage drug and alcohol abuse as an escape from the female's confusion of not being able to relate to men in a wholesome manner, all the while being strongly attracted to them by her DNA. She hasn't had the presence of a real Alpha Male in her life to model what one looks like. Even worse, daddy issues can lead to marital infidelity, which can be a real marriage killer. A woman's DNA wiring leads her to equate the male leader of her family unit with provision and protection. If they've been denied that during their early years it produces a lack of trust in the likelihood that the male's duties of provision and protection will be properly met without her intervention. If she has grown up in an environment where the father did not seem to provide for her safety and her provision of food, clothing and shelter, then, she will feel the need to become an Alpha Female. She is now disconnected from her biology – her DNA – and destruction of the male-female balance usually follows.

Once the female feels driven by the need to direct and control, she will attempt to assume and replace the male role. She will attempt to fill the vacuum. A normal male-female relationship at that point is a miraculous recovery – not impossible, but probably cannot be achieved without a lot of God's intervention. If you find her as a "damsel in distress," you may be just the *latest* Damsel Saver to come along in her life. She may require continual saving, leaving you unequally yoked, plowing in a circle, and beat down in the process.

The more aggressive and violent feminist movement that has surfaced over the last couple of decades is clearly a carefully laid plan of evil, aided and abetted by the inability or refusal of our culture to produce Alpha Males. The severe shortage of them has created an authority vacuum that women feel obligated to fill. They will try to fill it, even if it means operating completely outside their gifts and talents, and especially their DNA. It is to the shame of the Church that we've not been willing or capable of properly raising sufficient numbers of young men to take their places as the Alpha Males of this generation. As a result, young men are being taught by their experiences to operate in a "head-down" mode that draws a tight circle around oneself, afraid to venture outside it for fear of being criticized or publicly humiliated. Western culture now acts as if to be an Alpha Male is to be the worst of all the negative stereotypes that present-day feminism has to offer about men. The Church hasn't been contesting and refuting that accusation. It is blatant cowardice in the face of raw evil. The Church must step up and assume its proper role in raising young men with a backbone. Better to be a single Alpha Male than to be a married coward, raising more cowards. It's not a foot race you're struggling to win – the Lord has your back if you stay close. He will find your mate, but you must stay firm in your purpose. Be careful. You still have free will. He will warn you but He won't stop you from decisions with consequences you won't like.

For a woman, the best foundation for a healthy life-mate relationship is begun in a loving and trusting relationship with her earthly father. Her ability to fully believe that her father loves her and protects her is monumental in her development. Damage in that relationship spreads like ripples on a pond throughout her life. Substance abuse or other addictive behavior heaped on top of that is a multiplier for any other problems either of you can have. It's like gasoline poured onto that bonfire and just makes it that much harder to control the blaze, or survive it.

Problems With Your Wife

This may seem an oversimplification, and to many it may seem insulting, but if you're having problems with your wife, it's probably your fault. This assumes that you haven't joined into a marriage in haste, with a woman who is not spiritually and mentally prepared to be in a God-ordained marriage. This assumes an equally yoked, unified relationship underneath the Lord's covering. Remember back to the Garden of Eden? The leadership of the family, even if there are only two of you, belongs to the male. It's not because men are superior to women – it's because that's the way God planned it. He made the Alpha Male to be head of the family. But, if the army is starving, off course, or out of ammo, it's the general's fault, no excuses. Along with the authority and the finality of decisions, there comes consequence and the Alpha Male owns it all, for better or worse. The Alpha Male is the first line of defense in the family and must shoulder that responsibility, even if the family is only the two of you.

In the same sense, you are the first line of defense for your wife/family to make sense of the teachings that they receive from various sources, and judge their place in your lives. If you see something that doesn't line up with what the Lord has taught you, and you've proven out through study and prayer how you should consider the matter, then that line of thinking needs to be put aside – moved out of the way. It may even be that you come back to it, another day, and find a different meaning there that you didn't initially see or understand. If your wife is unhappy about your financial state of affairs and you're both students in college and don't have much, then the Alpha Male has an obligation to set the expectations of the family unit and avoid envy and frustration. Expectations tend to drive our understanding of what we have versus what we think we need. If you have young children, you and your wife may have made the decision that she will reduce or give up her work income. Your childcare situation may be such that it's more important to be home with them during those early years, than it is to have her income. That decision, even though made for all the right reasons will have consequences. Less money in the family budget means that our behavior has to change to accommodate that. We have to prepare ourselves to be able to handle those consequences without grumbling in our hearts. Our current culture runs after immediate gratification. Everyone wants everything, right now, whether they have earned it yet or not. Everyone has credit cards – right? Earning something through hard work is almost a forgotten art. Working is almost a forgotten art. Life doesn't usually just drop everything in our laps, but when our unmet desire for something overpowers our gratefulness for what we already have, we set the table for envy and gluttony. This can quickly degrade into the lust for things, simply to have them.

> *"When you ask, you do not receive, because you ask with wrong motives, that you may spend what you get on your pleasures"* (James 4:3).

The King James Version is a little more explicit – *"that ye may consume it upon your lusts."* Everyone knows what *that* means, even if we don't like hearing it.

> *"But if you harbor bitter envy and selfish ambition in your hearts, do not boast about it or deny the truth. Such 'wisdom' does not come down from heaven but is earthly, unspiritual, demonic. For where you have envy and selfish ambition, there you find disorder and every evil practice"* (James 3:14-16).

Priest of the Home

The Alpha Male and his mate endeavor to be in agreement and reach it through a variety of channels. In the raising of children, finances, career moves, etc., the couple is in a continual dance of discussion and observation, sharing hopes and dreams, with the goal of agreement on all things. All of these decisions are approached with prayer and listening to God, seeking good counsel when needed, and using the wisdom we've gained along the way. The goal is to arrive at a solution or decision that meets both of your needs. There are times when agreement doesn't quite come together and an impasse forms – gridlock. Sometimes it's because the answer is just slower in coming than we would like. Other times it's because there is a difference of perspective on the matter, or because there is a third, better choice, that has not yet been revealed. But, in matters of life and the family the final decision must lie with the Alpha Male and he will answer to the Lord for it all. This is not something to be taken lightly, or to assume that it makes you special and her not special. It means that, as the Alpha Male, at the moment of a required decision, you have to choose that path, knowing that the authority rests with you, even when you may not want it. Pray to God that you've heard it right.

None of this should be construed to suggest that women are not capable of positions of leadership in the Church. It also does not suggest that women cannot be in a position of leadership in business. In addition, women are just as capable of hearing God's voice as men are. If you're both hearing His voice through the Holy Spirit then you know that He will guide you both to the same conclusions on matters of the marriage and the family. You can rest assured that He won't be telling you things that violate the manner in which He has established marriage.

Every man needs another man to bounce things off of and from whom he can get good counsel. But, it can be very difficult to give specific advice to another man, unless he's asking you if he should get a divorce – the first answer is "no." Any subsequent answer to that question has to be prefaced with a lot of other questions about what has already been tried and what happened with that. But, men need that network of fellow believers that encourage and pray for each other. The complexity of our own lives is sometimes overwhelming. To attempt to understand the complexities of another man's life and family, and offer profound advice, is almost unthinkable without a direct intervention from the Holy Spirit to see past all of someone else's noise and confusion. In addition, hearing from God when operating in His permissive will can be more challenging than when operating in His perfect will. To help our understanding of permissive will versus perfect will, let's look at that moment when God told Abraham that he would destroy Sodom and Gomorrah. Abraham quickly entered into a bit of negotiating with God over whom and how much would be destroyed, based on how many righteous men he could find there. He was attempting to move that decision over into God's permissive will. For a while, Abraham did appear to be successful in his bid to save Lot's hometown, but ultimately, their sin was so great that God had had enough, setting into motion His "perfect" will which then prevailed over His "permissive" will. Abraham should not have felt as if he had failed in his attempt to persuade God in his actions. It is noteworthy that not only did Abraham feel able to request a different outcome, but that God considered it and agreed. Shortly afterwards, behavior by those in the city was so intolerable that God went back to His original decision to destroy it. I feel confident that Abraham saw that even though he might have hoped for a different outcome that the Lord took the correct course and that was that.

I propose that there is something to be considered here in looking at parents and their children, in regard to our permissive will versus our perfect will. I want them to eat the dinner I've prepared, but I don't want to micromanage their lives. I want them to use godly principles and I want them to hear God's voice about where to stand and to watch what He's doing there so they can be willing servants and be His hands and conduits of His love. But, I'm not going to make them into a mini-me and try to create in their lives what I've not done to my satisfaction in my own. If I try and micromanage their lives with my perfect will, what will become of them when I'm no longer there to do that for them? Not only is it a vain and self-centered approach to one's children, it's a collision course with God's perfect will for their lives. I have to be ready with my permissive will to accommodate who God made them to be that I haven't even discovered, yet. But, while they are living within my household there are hard limits as to what kind of moral behavior I'll tolerate from them. That would be the area of my perfect will.

While it falls to the Alpha Male to be the last ditch in hard decisions that affect the family, it can be a not very fun place to be. That's especially true when the "rational" course can seem so obvious to outside observers and opinion-givers, of which you may have many. When you're peaceful but those watching and offering advice become exasperated, there is plenty of opportunity for armchair quarterbacking. You have to know that you're making that decision the way you are because you are confident in God to pull it off – not in yourself to pull it off. The Alpha Male has faith in his God-given gifts, talents and anointing to accomplish what God has placed before him. It may seem to non-believers, those with little faith, or one not walking in the Spirit, that this confidence is in the man. But, that would be a misunderstanding. The Alpha Male's confidence is in the Lord. Jesus' disciples were a great example of this. They didn't claim that the miracles they performed originated with them. They always insisted that they were merely conduits, through which God's intent, direction and power flowed according to His good pleasure, because of their desire to serve Him.

Speak Life Into Your Wife

The active channel of faith is prayer and declaration. The Lord wants you to pray, and to declare His promises. He wants us to speak life. It's not because He has no idea what we want or need, *"for your Father knows what you need before you ask Him" (Matthew 6:8b)*. Knowing that the power of life and death is in the tongue, He wants us to speak those words of life in order to breathe into them His power and authority – the power of life. Speak life. Use the authority God gives you as priest of the home to build the strength of your marriage. Remember, we are free-will beings, created by God to make our life choices in whatever way we want. He wants us to choose life, but it's not something He forces on us.

> *"Again, truly I tell you that if two of you on earth agree about anything they ask for, it will be done for them by my Father in heaven" (Matthew 18:19).*

Husbands and wives – the two of you can agree that your marriage is blessed and protected by God. You can agree that it matters to God. Agree that it matters to your children. Agree as often as you can with God about your life, why you have one, and who you are. Speak it out. Speak it into the air. Give your words life. Give your words authority. Give them power through agreement with the Holy Spirit. Speak life into your wife and your family. Then, do it, again.

> *"Therefore put on the full armor of God, so that when the day of evil comes, you may be able to stand your ground, and after you have done everything, to stand" (Ephesians 6:13).*

He says you're going to need armor. You're going to be attacked. Don't be surprised like you hadn't heard about it. Your words stand guard on the front lines of your family.

While you're speaking life to your wife, make sure you're speaking life into your children, as well. Children need to see their parents live out their confidence in God to heal, to re-unite, to forgive, to bless. They need to see and hear their parents declaring and praying out loud, with confidence, declaring joy, healing and provision over the family. The prayers of parents need to be different every time they pray, demonstrating that it is not a memory recitation for mealtimes and goodnight prayers. It's a conversation with God. Teach them to pray with their hearts rather than with their tongues. The time of day has no bearing on when they can pray. Your prayers should include gratitude and a declaration of God's power and authority. Praying is timeless and should be a continual activity in our day. When children see and hear their parents pray it is a powerful thing in their lives. It has meaning instead of form, and an expectation of good from a good God, instead of a ritual-centered exercise that we do on a schedule.

Your Wife is Your Garden

Marriage isn't something you do in a vacuum. If you married right, you've married a real woman who is equally yoked with you – she lives in that single skin with you. She believes God for who she is and knows Jesus as Lord and Savior. She has the Holy Spirit. She is not clueless. The woman who knows who she is and how she's made is a self-confident woman. A self-confident woman will be able to use the fruit of the Spirit to overrule her emotions. Well, mostly, but not always. Women are more apt to use emotion than men when faced with difficult decisions. From a humorous angle, a woman might run in fear from a very large, angry animal, while a man might be thinking, "Cookout tonight and food for days!" I think that part of the reason for that behavior is that women are wired to be compassionate – caregivers. God put them in the position of carrying, birthing and nurturing the offspring of the family. Through the marriage, the Alpha Male can learn to increase his empathy and compassion, and his Bride can learn to pursue more wisdom. But, she is looking to you for leadership. If you don't provide it, and do it properly, she could possibly be lured away by other voices who sing to her about how she should step up and be the one calling the shots, making the important decisions without your input or leadership. After all, you don't seem to be doing it. Tending to your wife and reassuring her through good communication and in loving her strongly helps her to look to you as that provider and protector. A garden that isn't tended will become choked with weeds and in due time, be unworkable and non-productive. You have to spend the time necessary to see to it that your wife is able to be confident and content with your life together and your portion as a family. She needs to know that her Alpha Male will protect her heart as well as her physical being.

Man-Pleasing Spirit

One of the problems I've noticed frequently in marriages is that there is a temptation to be reverentially sweet and kind to everyone but each other. It seems that we feel the need to be "kindly judged" by those around us – it makes us feel good – but that one person closest to us gets unloaded on to make up for us holding it in the rest of the time. Behind closed doors it becomes a free-fire zone and the spouse is the easiest and most available target, and there's no one there to get in the way of it or witness it. Once started it is very damaging and becomes more so the longer it continues. The root of it is a man-pleasing spirit – that longing to be liked and appreciated, without much regard for the real cost. It is a nasty spirit that will steal from your family and erode the respect you have for each other. When you see it in yourself or your spouse, you need to move quickly and gently to remove its power from your lives. The antidote is respect, and rejection of the man-pleasing spirit, accompanied by the realization that your spouse gets the best of what you have to offer in this world. The Alpha Male knows that his spouse learns quickly by example. He has to lead this. She gets the best – *your* best. You will also be getting her best as she follows your lead. She is an amplifier of what is going on in your marriage. Make sure what you're putting into it is what you want to see come out, multiplied times ten. Women are very good at making many from one. Your spouse is the recipient of protection, blessing, loving, and plenty of fun to go along with it. Your most pleasant times in your lives should be with each other.

Divorce

"Every...household divided against itself will not stand." – Jesus.

Great care should be taken in deciding how to proceed when one of the marriage partners decides to abandon the relationship. You're supposed to be living in that same skin. Extricating yourself from it is not only a really bad idea, but it's going to rip some things apart and do a lot of damage. If that relationship was never a real marriage in the sight of God, and children are a part of that relationship, then that couple has ventured, knowingly or not, into territory reserved for real marriages. Being without God in a marriage is almost double lost-ness, with all the mess that comes with being lost, multiplied by the number of people in the family. A family full of lost souls is a spiritual train wreck, happening again and again. It may be buried beneath financial successes that mask the reality and buy our way out of some surface-level problems, but the interior reality always comes home, someday. But, lost-ness is not a good reason for divorce. If the man is not a believer and his wife is, her behavior is a witness to him of the power of God. That doesn't mean he gets to beat her up and degrade her. She is not a doormat, or property, or anything less than you. She is a Daughter of God. He sees how you're treating her.

God has already stated that He hates divorce. Divorce is the destruction of unity, and the God of All Creation is a big proponent of unity. Divorce stops two people from finding out whom they can become. You owe your mate your best efforts on their behalf – in education, spiritual and mental training, life experiences, love and adoration that unfetter and unbind them to bloom and blossom into children of the King and His Kingdom. All of that is cut short, maimed, and usually destroyed by divorce.

> "'The man who hates and divorces his wife," says the LORD, the God of Israel, 'does violence to the one he should protect,' says the LORD Almighty" (Malachi 2:16).

If there are children, divorce deprives them of an amazingly abundant life experience of watching the two most important people in their entire world begin to recall who they are, remember what God has given them, and turn it all around to accomplish recovery, growth and all of those magnificent blessings yet to come. And, the children are able to witness how their parents returned to what God has taught them and managed to restore their relationship. It can be a powerful and important tool in their character growth to learn and understand how to mend a relationship and return it to health, rather than give it over to the ravages of divorce and a broken home life that leaves deep scars in each of their lives.

Marriage is a microcosm that the Lord gives us to peer into something that doesn't happen anywhere else on this earth outside of the Church – the UNITY that God supports as a pillar of His Kingdom. Bless, encourage and enrich each other, knowing that you'll both share in every bit of it.

Chapter 15 – Unity and Intimacy – The Church

I spoke earlier of the Shema:

"Shema Yisrael Adonai Eloheinu Adonai Echad."

What I did not mention at that moment was something that may seem heretical to some, even blasphemous. The word "echad," the last word of the phrase, in Hebrew has multiple meanings, depending on context. Frequently it means "one" as in counting. If there is a "one" then there must also be a "two," or even another "one," and so forth. The actual and best translation of that word when not counting something is "unified," or "unity."

"Hear, O' Israel, The Lord God is Unified (Unity)."

All of a sudden, that phrase can lead us somewhere we didn't know it was going. Consider the word "unity" and its place in God's Word. If you were to go through the Bible and look for every time it spoke of unity, or "one another," or being "one," you would find that it shows up a lot. It seems to me that unity is pretty important to God. Jesus addressed this directly in this passage concerning his disciples:

> *"My prayer is not for them alone. I pray also for those who will believe in me through their message, that all of them may be one, Father, just as you are in me and I am in you. May they also be in us so that the world may believe that you have sent me. I have given them the glory that you gave me, that they may be one as we are one— I in them and you in me—so that they may be brought to complete unity. Then the world will know that you sent me and have loved them even as you have loved me" (John 17:20-23).*

Looking carefully through those verses we see, *"you are in me and I am in you,"* and *"so that they may be brought to **complete unity.***" Not only that, but note that He says *"May they also be in us."* These are very strong words and should not be glossed over or taken lightly. There is a powerful message here that might be a bit scary to some – but it shouldn't be. It should be exciting that He cares so much for you and me that He has plans for us that we can't even begin to fathom. But, He's trying to give you hints and aspirations that lead you in the direction He wants.

> *"...no one knows the thoughts of God except the spirit of God. What we have received is not the spirit of the world, but the Spirit who is from God... This is what we speak, not in words taught us by human wisdom but in words taught by the Spirit, explaining spiritual realities with Spirit-taught words" (1 Corinthians 2:11b,12a – 13).*

This whole concept has been a bit of an answer to a very thorny theological question I've had regarding our relationship with God. Jesus spoke often of those who are God's "servants" and used servant analogies many times in his messages to the Jewish community. Yet,

Jesus ultimately told his followers that His preference is that we graduate to become "friends," rather than servants. That's pretty strong stuff if you really ponder its meaning.

> *"I no longer call you servants, because a servant does not know his master's business. Instead, I have called you friends, for everything that I learned from my Father I have made known to you" (John 15:15).*

For many years I've wrestled with the understanding that God wants an "intimate relationship" with His children. Yet, when I consider the basis for an intimate relationship, there is no place for that kind of relationship between a servant and a master. To have an intimate relationship means that there is equality in the relationship – in *some* fashion. Our ability to become intimate with God appears to be solely dependent upon the indwelling of the Holy Spirit. Through the Holy Spirit, God is beckoning us to become "friends." Even beyond that He wants us to be restored as "sons and daughters." He even tells us to call him "Daddy." THAT is the relationship that God wants with us – a staggering fact. For many of us that is the moment to turn and run, as the Israelites did, in fear of the idea of being in that kind of relationship with the most awesome power of all.

God's intent was always a personal relationship with His favorite creation. Moses invited everyone to come hear from the Lord, but they begged off saying that it was too scary to consider and that Moses should go take notes and come back and tell them what God said. Hearing from God was just too dicey and probably pretty dangerous. Yet, here we are, being rejoined into the family, restored to the Father, from a state of corruption and fallen mankind, to being on family terms with the Father – Melech Ha'Olam – King of the Universe. What do we need in order to become friends? Jesus tells us that you need to

The Alpha Male

learn from Him what He learned from the Father. That's a pretty tall order. How can we do that?

I believe it requires us to not only hear God's voice, but to take what He says and put it into action, stepping out in faith – using His faith – that He will be there to meet us. Loving His other children is one of the biggies in that learning process. I must confess that the biggest challenges in my life are wrapped up in loving God's other children. It's easy to love my own children. Heck, God puts that into my DNA to start with. And, some people are just plain lovable – at least much of the time. But, how do I manage to really love His *other* children – especially those that don't *act* very lovable?

"I'm not always easy to love." I spoke those words at the memorial service for Herman Neusch; a beautiful heart of a man who was a lifeline God threw me as a wedding present when I married my wife, Esta. Her father, Paw-Paw Herman Neusch, was right up front, fun, God-loving, spirit-filled, and a shock to me after so much anguish in my life, and a badly failed first marriage. Over the decades I knew him, he was the most approachable and loving man I have ever met. He spoke to my heart and touched it in ways I didn't know were still possible. He became the loving father I had not ever really had. If he knew I wasn't always easy to love, he never let me know about it. He would hug me and kiss me on the cheek and tell me he loved me, and that he was so proud of me. I had never heard words spoken like that to me. He was always encouraging and positive, and I got to the point where I started believing him. Paw-Paw was an Alpha Male. I learned a lot about being an Alpha Male from him. I love my boys. I try to treat them like that, but I never had another adult treat me like that. It was heaven-sent assistance in rebuilding my understanding of who I am – a child of God – loved and cherished in ways I can't even comprehend.

John H. Ingle

Unity of the Church

I believe that the Father's heart is that His Church becomes unified and acts in unity. The Rabbi Gamaliel, a highly esteemed teacher of the Law, warned his fellow members of the Sanhedrin that if Jesus' disciples were acting only on their own as men, then their efforts would come to nothing. But, if what they were doing was from God *"you will only find yourselves fighting against God" (Acts 5:39b).* That's pretty strong stuff, and scary, too. Imagine for a moment finding ourselves, as believers, *"fighting against God."* Yet, today many within the Church are raising up a destructive cycle of judgment of other Christians and other Christian pastors, leaders, and churches, ready to pick apart everything they say and do. You can use an internet search engine and put almost any Christian leader's name in it and come up with multiple websites that excoriate that leader as a "false teacher," or even worse, a "devil worshipper." Some isolated statement or offhand comment they made is magnified and distorted to become an unforgiveable crime against the Kingdom of God and their head is required on a platter.

> *"You, then, why do you judge your brother or sister? Or why do you treat them with contempt? For we will all stand before God's judgment seat" (Romans 14:10).*

It is easy and very earthly to cast stones from afar, but it's also an awful perversion of God's purpose for His Church. If one of His followers makes too much money for your taste, then ignore it. If they preach too much healing and miracles for the reality you enjoy, find something else to do. If they have too long of a worship service and people are dancing in the aisles, and that offends you, don't attack the pastor or his church – just don't go there. Do they celebrate Christmas as Jesus' birthday, but you're convinced it's leftovers from a long-ago pagan holiday, and should *not* be celebrated? If you think Easter is just an invention that began from a pagan celebration, if they celebrate Easter does that make them pagans? Go to God and ask Him why you're offended by His children. Ask Him if there's an income limit for a Christian. Ask Him if He's ever made someone wealthy because He likes what they do with the money they've been given. Ask Him if David dancing wildly, half-naked in the street, was offensive to Him. Just be prepared to stick around long enough to actually hear His answer, and not the answer on the internet that someone has worked hard to sell you. Take His answer deep into your heart and dwell on it.

The process of judgment is designed to arrive at a verdict – innocent, or guilty. It's a dangerous place to go, to launch ourselves headlong into arriving at a verdict regarding a fellow believer. Anyone trying to get there by using their rational mind is almost assuredly making a terrible mistake. We must all remember that if we are offended by what a fellow Christian is doing in their good faith, it may be that we don't actually have the fullness of the Holy Spirit and need to ask for it. It's also important to ask whether we even *need* to understand them from God's perspective. God's ultimate plan isn't up for a vote and He doesn't run everything by us to see how we feel about it. Without the Holy Spirit indwelling, much of what we see and hear isn't ever going to make sense. Our rational minds are *not* what the Lord uses to run His Kingdom. His idea of order and our idea of order could be different in ways we cannot even begin to imagine.

> *"The person without the Spirit does not accept the things that come from the Spirit of God but considers them foolishness, and cannot understand them because they are discerned only through the Spirit. The person with the Spirit makes judgments about all*

> *things, but such a person is not subject to merely human judgments"* (1 Corinthians 2:14-15).

It clearly states that a person with the Spirit makes judgments about all *things*, not all *people*. The apostle Paul was, in his own words, behaving as practically a perfect Jew – *"in regard to the law, a Pharisee; as for zeal, persecuting the church; as for righteousness based on the law, faultless"* (Philippians 3:5,6a). He was <u>*faultless*</u> in his righteousness – according to what he *knew*. Jesus changed all that on the road to Damascus and changed the entire world at the same time. Paul cautions us:

> *"And if on some point you think differently, that too God will make clear to you"* (Philippians 3:15b).

The degree of assault on fellow believers seems to be the most intense where the Holy Spirit is moving the most notably. What we do NOT need to do is throw on the robe of the Judge and begin our crawl into the Holy Seat of God to render our final judgment. The apostle Paul warns us that:

> *"If you bite and devour each other, watch out or you will be destroyed by each other"* (Galatians 5:14-15).

My own life has some pretty unusual circumstances and events. I'm sure some will be tempted to blame it all on drug-induced hallucinations or fantasy, much as they might accuse the prophet Daniel. But, I have no reason to believe anything other than what the Lord has shown me and told me. These events are real and have transpired as I have described. When I hear directly from God, I would be a complete and utter fool if I didn't take it very seriously. If you have an issue with anything I've related here, I suggest that you refer to Paul and attempt to acknowledge that, perhaps, *"that too God will make clear to you."* All I can do is relay what He's told me and remind you – *"the stones"* – they are still coming. Do you really want to ignore His warning because you think you have a lock on what God will do and not do? Was the parting of the Red Sea just an imaginary tale that makes for a good Bible story? Did Jesus really raise the dead, or is that just another good story? Picture yourself as Ezekiel, staring out over a valley battleground of dry human bones as the Lord asks you:

> *"Son of man, can these bones live?"* I said, *"Sovereign* Lord, *you alone know"* (Ezekiel 37:3).

Ezekiel was a very smart guy. He knew that if the Lord wanted those bones to live that nothing in Heaven or on Earth could stop it. Indeed, *"Lord, You alone know."* And, He did and He still does. Whatever you decide, Lord – that's what's going to happen. The Lord God stood up an entire army from those bones in front of Ezekiel to prove His point. Note that God did *not* speak to the bones. *He told Ezekiel what to say and had him prophesy to the bones.* The bones responded to the words Ezekiel spoke. We have to stop pretending that we can decide what God can or can't do, or will or won't do. That is the height of vanity to pretend that we can decide that for God. We have to stop judging His Church – His children – and learn to accommodate someone in it besides ourselves and people that look and act exactly like us. There are hands and feet and noses and thumbs and everything else of a body in the church. We don't all look the same and do the same things, but I'm not ready to start cutting off my limbs because they don't look or act like my eyes. If we're afraid of the Holy Spirit and keep our distance, then we're going to be offended and afraid of what God is doing in His Church.

At this moment I think it's necessary to revisit something I showed you earlier in this book that the Lord put right in front of me several times.

> "...In the last times there will be scoffers who will follow their own ungodly desires.' These are the people who divide you, who follow mere natural instincts and do not have the Spirit. But you, dear friends, by building yourselves up in your most holy faith and praying in the Holy Spirit, keep yourselves in God's love as you wait for the mercy of our Lord Jesus Christ to bring you to eternal life. Be merciful to those who doubt; save others by snatching them from the fire; to others show mercy, mixed with fear—hating even the clothing stained by corrupted flesh" (Jude 1: 17-22).

Take extreme care that you don't find yourself in the first group He is describing. He's talking about people *IN the body*. *"These are the people who divide you...and do not have the Spirit."* It's not *our* Church, it's His Church. So keep yourself *"in the Holy Spirit...keep yourselves in God's love...snatch them* (non-believers) *from the fire...*(and) *to others show mercy..."* Bring lots of mercy, and let's all leave the judgment of Jesus' Bride in some ditch, somewhere along the way. He'll do all the judging, soon enough.

What Does God Say?

Intimacy suggests a give-and-take that is borne of equality and a ready willingness to yield in favor of the other when the other makes an earnest request. Intimacy is soft and open to the heart of the other. It is a state of mind – a state of the spirit. It is not intended to be shared with others who don't share in that relationship. Does that stand the test of *"do unto others?"* Is the equality factor the reason God sent Jesus – we are the grafted branch and share the vine in the same manner as the original branches – is intimacy with God only possible through His son? Is that the extended meaning of "no one comes to the Father but through me."? Are we able to be directly intimate with God? Is He too much to bear, even if we are His children? If we are able to be directly intimate, what is that pathway and the example we can follow? Certainly Moses would qualify (*"with him I speak face to face"*). If we are not able, we should not presume the ability.

God says that:

> "As the heavens are higher than the earth, so are my ways higher than your ways and my thoughts than your thoughts" (Isaiah 55:9).

But, if we will endeavor to understand what He knows we *can* understand, or at least receive His ways, and instill within ourselves the understanding that His way is going to be best, then His way is going to be what *we* want. Then, when we pray for our earnest desires, we're really not praying for our personally generated desires, or *wants* (usually lusts), but the desires we learned from Him. So, if you've been disappointed in your prayers, perhaps you're not praying for His desires, but your own. I think prayer works like that. Jesus brings us unity with God, independent of equality. Intimacy unites us, *"that they may be one as we are one…so that they may be brought to complete unity"* (John 17:22a, 23b).

God is looking at you, saying, "I want you to be like Joseph, with his skills of prophecy, interpretation, government and organization…but more. I want you to be like David, with vast strength of mind, courage and a heart of worship…but more. I want you to have access to Me like Moses…but more. I want you to carry the authority and power that I placed in Elijah...but more. You are sons and daughters of The Most High God." He wants you to learn to behave as such.

The Bible tells us that David is a man after God's own heart:

> *"'I have found David son of Jesse, a man after my own heart; he will do everything I want him to do'"* (Acts 13:22b).

Imagine for a moment and understand if you can, that He would love to say the same thing about you. God is calling us to use Jacob's ladder – the ladder that the Holy Spirit provides us to climb above the clouds and take a walk through the constellations and galaxies of the universe and see across the billions of years of time – infinity – and take a longer view of life and purpose. You could worry and fret and say that this invites us to become prideful in ourselves. But, He wants us to elevate way beyond the earthly snare of pride, casting Satan's temptations and empty promises aside in full favor of a view of Creation that says that I have all these things through the Holy Spirit and there are no human feelings of how cool I am or am not – it just *IS!* And, that's how God wants it. We become conduits of God's desires made real. We share in that through being part of the holy vessel of the Bride of Christ

The apostle Paul tells us that we can know the thoughts of God through the Holy Spirit. Not only that, but that we can speak what we hear through the Spirit. We can hear *"spiritual truths in spiritual words."* These are not my words. They are in your Bible. Do you believe it? Our ability to become intimate with God is solely dependent upon the indwelling of the Holy Spirit and our uplifting of that Spirit in our lives. The goal is that His ways become our ways. There is no replacement or substitute. It is what He wants from the Church.

The Alpha Male

Connection

The human mind was designed for group activity. It is often within the regular bonding of the group in a worship and study atmosphere that the brain has the opportunity to learn and re-learn – to gain wisdom. The Lord wants us to use these settings to heal from our wounded states, internalizing His ethics and emotional state. When we retreat to our inner selves is when we cut off that group learning that allows us to internalize our new or re-learned knowledge and understanding of our world. Being part of a group is important. What that group does and thinks becomes part of us. Making that a good thing is critical to both healing and growth.

Here's a science experiment for you (don't try this at home). Eat nothing but biscuits and water for weeks and months and go to the gym, regularly, while you're doing that. What you'll find is that you will begin to tear down existing tissue (catabolism) to recover the ingredients to make needed new tissue. Continue to do this and you will eventually start destroying your internal organs. And, then you will die. A similar thing happens in the spirit – connection is nutrition. A lack of connection with the body of believers leaves the spirit weak and under-nourished and much more ready to make bad decisions from a position of weakness. If you cut yourself off from connection with the Church Body *and* the Spirit, your spirit will wither and you may die a much worse death.

The Alpha Male is a spiritual being living in a physical body, and connection is something the Lord has created for you so that you are nourished in your soul. *"Do unto others,"* is all over the New Testament. There's a really good reason for that. The Lord rates unity very highly. The Lord has founded Creation on relationship. Just look at all the complex relationships that exist throughout what He's made, from insects, up through primates. All Creation hums with relationships, from the ants of the ground to the bees of the air. It is crucial that you are connected to the Church Body. It is where you are nourished, nourish others, grow, feel loved and fit in. If you are in a Church body where this isn't happening, either you're in the wrong place or your heart is. Figure out which one it is, and fix it. It *is* that important.

The God Committee

Over the years there has been a lot of teaching within the Church about "discipling" and being accountable to others in your life. Those are all good concepts that can be taken down the wrong path and end up being a religion committee that takes the place of God in your personal life. I'm reminded of Joseph, after having been sold into slavery by his brothers and on his way to Egypt. How many people were in a position of spiritual authority in his life? I would hazard the guess that there was no one other than God Himself. Who in pagan Egypt would have been able to be his guidance counselor?

I find in my own life that primary accountability has to always go back to the Lord God who gives me breath and meets me in my life, every day that I invite Him. He counsels, guides, and invites me to His call and purpose. But, I have to invite Him. I have personally experienced so many instances of the God Committee taking someone off the path and making them accountable to a consensus, that the whole concept makes me, perhaps, overly cautious. The religion committee is not the same thing as connection. There is a mythical story of the camel being a race horse designed by a committee. It won't win a normal horse race but it can go for days without water, while carrying several people. Good design, but it's the right answer to the wrong problem. A committee typically has authority to "make it so," whether it's actually

The Alpha Male

a good idea, or not. Committees are a group-think phenomenon that can strike dead-center on the target of mediocrity and "safety." Safety is when no one steps out and believes that God will be there to meet them. David stepped out to face Goliath. The religion committee would have advised trying to negotiate a treaty, instead. Safety is when Noah takes the idea of building the Ark to a committee and they all vote it down as being surely something the Lord would never ask to be done, and it's not even raining. Noah didn't go to the committee and ask if that was really such a good idea. They would have laughed him out of the room…oh, wait, they *did* laugh him out of the room. God gave Noah the direction and the task to accomplish. Now, if Noah needed further guidance from Man on that matter he could go to the committee and ask where he could get some really nice tall, straight trees.

Being accountable to one or more spiritual authority figures in your life requires that they be tuned into God in a very strong fashion, in ways that acknowledge that your relationship with God is not their relationship with God. They can serve as bar ditches, fence lines, and warning signs, but not as a foam-lined, enforced spiritual box.

Who was David's committee – the Mighty Men? Probably not. They were all fearsome warriors but they didn't seem to have the spiritual bent and depth that David had, at least not by what we're told about them. They were more inclined to obey David, without question, and usually did, even going so far as to send the husband of a beautiful woman to the very front of the front lines where he would die. They reported back, dutifully, that the husband was no more and it was now safe to go appropriate the ex-warrior's wife. Notice that none of them tried to stop him, or even suggest that it might be all that great an idea. That doesn't sound like the quality of spiritual guidance you want from your mighty men. It's probably not a good idea to get counsel from someone who depends on you for their well-being. Beware of the sources of your guidance and their capabilities. Fortunately for David, he did have the prophet Nathan, who was a close advisor. He probably wished that he had listened a little better to Nathan on some topics.

Chapter 16 – Conscience & Who You Are

A Clear Conscience and Being Whole

The hesitant heart – one that is obstructed by guilt, or self-doubt – is very similar to the unrepentant heart, which makes one into the "double-minded man."

> *"...because the one who doubts is like a wave of the sea, blown and tossed by the wind. That person should not expect to receive anything from the Lord. Such a person is double-minded and unstable in all they do"* (James 1:6b-8).

Guilt is a weighty stain where you should have a clear conscience that allows you to be able to approach the throne room as sons and daughters. A very popular method of dealing with sin these days is to go straight from conviction to being forgiven without having to pass through repentance and a change in our behavior. Our excuse is we're/they're "good people."

Guilt and self-doubt are pandemic in Christian culture. We are taught to be humble, but we replace that with destructive timidity, rather than humility. Humility means you're "listening and able to take instruction." Timidity means we might know what to do but we're afraid to do it. We discount ourselves and badmouth ourselves. We hover at the edge of condemning ourselves as unworthy of even being saved, as if we shouldn't be. Much of what ails our society and exposes fallen man in America is the self-loathing of a people who reject God but haven't figured out what to do with their guilt for doing so.

> *"For since the creation of the world God's invisible qualities—his eternal power and divine nature—have been clearly seen, being understood from what has been made, so that people are without excuse" (Romans 1:20).*

When *"people are without excuse,"* they are keenly aware of it even if they don't allow the knowledge to come forth from their inner being. Then, guilt comes and makes its home. God tells us that we need to give forgiveness in order to receive it. But, then we turn around to those we've injured and say, "Sorry – not sorry," keeping and nursing the anger and guilt through a fake exercise that we pretend is going to free us, but does not. The double-minded man then continues to testify against us and we are weak and sick, and still carry our guilt.

Before receiving the Lord's Supper, *"Everyone ought to examine themselves before they eat of the bread and drink from the cup" (1 Corinthians 11:28).* Not only do we need to understand what we are receiving, we're to do it with a clear heart, unencumbered by the weight of guilt and shame. We have to let it go. And, when we bring our gifts to the Lord and you remember *"that your brother or sister has something against you, leave your gift there in front of the altar. First go and be reconciled to them; then come and offer your gift" (Matthew 5:23-24).* He wants you to bring your gift to Him with a full heart, lacking any guilt or anger, so that you can be blessed in doing it. It's for *you* that you do this.

There are so many in the Church that can't seem to part with the guilt of the old man we once were. We don't leave it at the cross. Too often we cling to it as a part of our "humility" not realizing that we rob ourselves of the power God expects us to use to witness salvation to His lost children and "snatch them from the fire." And, it's not *our* power, it's *His* power – we are the delivery mechanism He has appointed to get it done – His Creation delivering the good news to the rest of His Creation.

> *"Dear friends, if our hearts do not condemn us, we have confidence before God" (1 John 3:21).*

Put off being double-minded, so that you can be who God has restored you to be. The "world" in the physical plane will always be trying to exert its influence. Don't go along with it. If pride rears its ugly head, don't go along with it, either. People love to find other people to praise and elevate as heroes. If, for some act or idea, you find men praising you, don't let it rest on you and tempt you to luxuriate in it as if you were the rightful destination of that praise. Your refusal to let the praise rest on you can become a learning moment for those who are tempted to praise what "man" is doing. Push the praise right on up to where it belongs – the Author and Finisher of our faith, and make sure they see you doing it, as a witness and blessing to them.

Healing – Body and Spirit

The Church also too often rejects healing as something for sissies or cowards – we're *supposed* to suffer. If we're not suffering we're not good Christians. Many struggle with the memory of not being loved and cared for as children. Many abused children grow up with a certain knowledge that they are unlovable, and believe that their "defects" make that justifiably so. That emotion becomes the belief that we aren't worthy of living in a miracle of healing for others to witness and thereby glorify God. God doesn't *want* me to be joyful…oh, wait…He *does* want me to be joyful. The Bible is chock-full of encouragements to be joyful, as well as peaceful. The word shalom in Hebrew is often interpreted as, "Hi," "Bye," "Peace," "What's up," and several other generic greetings, but the root more closely approximates being "whole," in the sense of completeness. Thus, the greeting "Shalom aleykhem" instead of just saying "Peace to you," more literally is a blessing or encouragement of "Wholeness to you" (Jeff Benner). Imagine that for a moment – being whole – physically, spiritually and every other way possible, so that you lack for no good thing in your entire life.

> *"The* LORD *is my shepherd, I lack nothing. He makes me lie down in green pastures, He leads me beside quiet waters, He refreshes my soul" (Psalm 23:1-3).*

In the original Hebrew, this phrase could just as easily be, and possibly better translated, "The Lord tends me like a flock, providing me with the best – lush pastures, peaceful, sparkling water, and He returns me to a refreshed state." That doesn't sound like suffering and self-loathing, which is *not* to say that you will never suffer in this life. It also does not mean that you will never suffer for the gospel. But, suffering for the gospel is NOT the same thing as just suffering for suffering's sake. Suffering for suffering's sake is just self-destructive and pointless negativity that robs you of the power and authority in which God expects you to operate. It commits you to look and behave exactly like the double-minded man. Don't be drawn into believing that your prayers for physical healing are selfish, as if there is only so much healing to go around and perhaps others are more deserving than you. God is not sitting around comparing you to some other believer to see who deserves something more than the other one.

The Alpha Male

If we look at the earthly ministry of Jesus, we see someone who is healing continually, everywhere He went, of both physical and spiritual illness. We have to get over guilt and selfishness labels and start asking God for healings based on who God is. The big piece that seems often to be missing is the boldness of King David to move us into the throne room of God. There, we declare His might and glory and Jesus' victory over sin and death that Jesus tells us is the key to those prayers being answered – through *using* our faith – the faith we get from the Uncreated God – The Everlasting Father.

King David had great joy, great gratefulness, and great expectations of the Lord. The Lord knew that He was seeing great faith, and rewarded David for it, just as He had done for Abraham. I have come to believe that we don't ask with enough boldness, and that lack of boldness testifies to the weakness of our faith. It appears that the vast majority of us do not have faith the size of a grain of mustard seed. Otherwise, there would be things happening that clearly are not, that should be happening if we were bold and stouthearted in our confidence of what God will do when we ask with the right motive. Jesus told us that He does what He sees the Father doing. Let's get a lot better at seeing what the Father is doing. Only the Holy Spirit is able to show us that.

Peter and John were going up to the temple at the time of prayer and saw a man "lame from birth." The man asked them for money but, instead, they told him that they had neither silver nor gold but would share with them what they did have – the authority to declare his healing in the name of Jesus of Nazareth. The man responded by walking, leaping, and praising God. The crowds knew who this man was, were astonished, and came running to them. Peter asked the crowd why they were so surprised, as if they had done this by their own power or godliness, rather than through the power of God to glorify Jesus. A larger crowd gathered and both disciples spoke to the crowd and about five thousand were saved that day. The healing was a prelude to a much bigger event, in the same fashion that Jesus used healing. But, for that act the disciples were arrested and threatened by the temple authorities. They were then released and the two rejoined their fellow believers. Their fellow believers raised their voices in prayer.

> *"Now, Lord, consider their threats and enable your servants to speak your word with great boldness. Stretch out your hand to heal and perform signs and wonders through the name of your holy servant Jesus" (Acts 4:29-30).*

Immediately the place shook and they were all filled with the Holy Spirit and "spoke the word of God, boldly." I haven't been able to find any evidence that this request that was obviously granted, has ever expired, been canceled, or has been worn out because we used it too much. The healing that Peter and John had spoken into being was physical, and while it certainly must have had a spiritual effect on the man healed, it started with his body, but depended on his faith to receive. It can start with bodies today, too. God still heals bodies. We just need to figure out why it seems that we too often discount and devalue that act of mercy. I fully believe that it is primarily due to that timidity and self-doubt that we question whether we have any right to ask for such things, as if it were profanity or vanity to do so. Like King David, you can be humble and still have great confidence in God.

When the apostle Paul was preaching at Lystra he saw a lame man and *"saw that he had the faith to be healed,"* so Paul instructed him to *"Stand up on your feet!"* The man jumped up and began to walk. Paul saw, through the Holy Spirit, that the man had the confidence to believe God that this miracle was for him. As a result, he received that miracle – no timidity, no self-doubt – he just received it.

The Alpha Male

When the centurion came to Jesus on behalf of a suffering servant, Jesus offered to go to the servant and help. The centurion replied that he fully understood authority and he knew Jesus had it, so all He had to do was say the word and it would happen. Jesus was astonished and told those around Him that He had not found faith like this anywhere in Israel. Jesus turned to the centurion and said, *"Go! Let it be done just as you believed it would" (Matthew 8:13)*. I can practically see the big smile on Jesus' face as he said it. I'm sure Jesus already saw the centurion's faith and chose that moment to make a statement to the crowd. He was calling them out to *use* their faith, not just to *have* faith. The centurion used his faith without hesitation and spoke it aloud. The centurion was an Alpha Male. Jesus has essentially said He is giving us His power and authority, and wants us to go make Him proud of how we use it to bless His children and reach the lost. But, He also asked:

> *"However, when the Son of Man comes, will he find faith on the earth?" (Matthew 18:8b).*

That question should make you think. The need for *"snatching them from the fire"* comes to mind, and the faith that it will take to get that done. Many Christians believe He can. Jesus wants us to believe that He will.

Crossroads – Healing or Not?

When Peter and John met the crippled man as they were about to enter the temple, Peter told him, *"In the name of Jesus Christ of Nazareth, walk,"* and extended his hand to help the man rise to his feet. At that point the man "instantly" received his healing – at that moment he "walked into" his miracle – not days, or weeks or months later, but immediately. Unbelief is a miracle killer. The Bible tells us that when Jesus came to his hometown:

> *"...he began teaching the people in their synagogue..."* but, *"...he did not do many miracles there because of their lack of faith"* (Matthew 13:54b, 58).

The town's inhabitants thought they already knew who Jesus was. He was just another guy from the old neighborhood. Who cared what He had to say? He saw their immediate willingness to deny Him and so He gave them what they asked for – nothing. It makes me think of that vision of a prison cell where no one cared that I was there. I am fully convinced that through unbelief, denial or stubbornness we can refuse to walk in a God-given miracle and thereby not receive it. We can also be stubborn by insisting that the world somehow acknowledge our diligent and dedicated suffering first, before we would allow ourselves to receive what we need so badly. God refers to this as "the hardening of our hearts." We can actually insist that our diligent suffering is elevated and glorified before men before we might allow God to act. The miracle would then become our invention instead of God's and the credit for that miraculous intervention stolen away from Him as we attempt to "earn it." We are rewarded in the same way that Jesus rewarded his hometown. He won't force it on you.

From Heaven to Earth

God's existence is not a function of how well I think He's meeting my "needs" at the moment. If I feel like God is nowhere to be found, it's time to revisit the verse, *"But you (Lord) are holy, enthroned in the praises of Israel (his people)"* (Psalms 22:3). At the moment that the Lord seems to have vanished, it is perennially true that it is we who have vanished – abandoning the presence of the Lord God in favor of some sidetrack idea of pleasure or must-do work. The required work was all done at the cross. Everything from there on is fully owned by the God of all Creation. Feeling like God has left you off at the side of the road, somewhere, can be a really sad feeling. But, all too often we get something in our heads and we run off after it, firmly convinced that it's a great idea and God must surely approve. Now, where did He go? It's almost too much to ask, "Where did I go?" Now, I'm sad because things are crashing and burning and I'm not getting what I wanted and surely needed…sort of.

When we're not listening and not hearing God's voice, we start to become introspective, retreating into our rational mind that can't understand spiritual matters. From introspection, it's a short journey to negativity and the loss of peace and joy. The cure is first to listen and hear. The next thing to do is be thankful for what He has done for us. Dwell on it. Reverse course. I firmly believe that thankfulness – gratitude – is a towering truth in the life of the Alpha Male and his Bride. Without gratitude, we seem to be always at the edge of tasting loss – of not having enough. That manner of thinking can take you right into jealousy and longing for something that someone else has that you think they don't deserve, and maybe you should have it. The poverty spirit thrives on not having enough. The poverty spirit is neediness expressed through fear of lack. It keeps one's focus aimed inward. It disrupts our ability to worship and offer praise to the Everlasting Uncreated God. The assumption in the poverty spirit frame of mind is that there is only so much to go around. That means that anyone who is doing better than you are (according to your way of thinking), has taken your share as well as theirs. They have your gold, silver, cattle, or whatever. That is not God's style at all.

Several years ago my wife and I attended the Austin School of Supernatural Ministry (AUSSM) at True Life Fellowship in Round

Rock, Texas. The school is based on the methods and materials of the School of Supernatural Ministry at Bethel Church in Redding, California. It was a three year course that focused on hearing God and moving in prophecy and healing. The concept seems scary but is really quite simple. The student practices observation and listening to see what and who God is "highlighting." When He moves, we listen. Then, we give the word we heard to the one highlighted. Declaration of God's love and provision over others was also a key ingredient. It was a refreshing and activating lifestyle that brought a lot of things together in my life at once. The "word" given was always to build up – never to tear down, correct or punish. It is, indeed, supernatural to see so many people responding that the word they were given was exactly what was on their heart and mind and how grateful they were to receive it. They knew it was from God. There was no other explanation. God is so awesome.

My help comes from the Lord, not from man or his government, or the accuser. Satan has no authority over a believer that the believer does not give him. His only play is to get you to agree with him, just as he did with Eve in the garden. This is why God wants us to live *from* Heaven *to* earth, and not try to live in the physical, looking *towards* Heaven. This is part of why Jesus said, repeatedly, that the Kingdom of Heaven is at hand (upon you). This means that you don't have to live in the physical – you can live in the spirit while inhabiting this "vessel" that God has created for you, caring for it as part of the Lord's Holy Temple. Your literal nearness – living *in* the Kingdom of Heaven (towards earth) – is a preparatory step to living solely as a spiritual being in the Kingdom to come. God moves in our world when it suits Him. But, it appears that His preference is that we learn to move in His. This is your training ground for things to come – big things. Try to be ready.

The Alpha Male

Living "in the world" is to be the pinball, thrown to and fro by the actions and opinions of others. Pinball is the game of the world. To live from Heaven towards earth is to remove oneself from the world's game and believe the Lord God. Believe that He has created you to be sons and daughters, not pinballs for the world to abuse for their amusement. Not only that but also not to be thrown about *"by every wind of doctrine."* How do you stop the world from spinning out of control when you find yourself in the pinball game? You step out onto the knowledge of God and His authority in the Universe – not in vanity and self-importance – but, "seeing" the world through God's point of view. Then, your pathway becomes much more clear and your responsibility in it, as well. Once you've glimpsed that greater reality, your solutions jump into focus. Very often at that point, the Lord just sticks the solution right in front of us.

Who Are You...*Really?*

To be "whole" means that you have to know who you are – who you are in Christ. You are not trash; you are not junk; you are not worthless; you are not "nothing." Jesus did not die for "nothing." But, I believe that the Church gets so hung up on the possibility of pride and insufficient humility that we degrade ourselves and each other. We become afraid to be anything beyond the dirt from which we were originally created. You are an awesome creation of God, upon whom he has bestowed free will – "fearfully and wonderfully made" – love Him or don't, it's up to you. However, repentance and acceptance of the sacrifice that restores our souls as sons and daughters is also a free will choice that we must make. But, that is how we are restored to the Father, through repentance and acceptance of the sacrifice, made in our place.

John H. Ingle

It's very popular these days to get your DNA tested and find your bloodlines of heritage. But, your DNA is not who you are. It describes the mechanics of how your bodysuit is assembled and where its bloodline has been, historically, not your character, or who you are in Christ.

Who are you? You are:

1. Fearfully and wonderfully made (Psalm 139:14)
2. A new creation (2 Corinthians 5:17)
3. God's messengers of reconciliation (2 Corinthians 5:18)
4. A child of God (John 1:12)
5. The light of the world (Matthew 5:14a)
6. Heirs of God, Joint heirs with Christ (Romans 8:17)
7. Seated in the heavenlies with Christ (Ephesians 2:6)
8. God's temple (1 Corinthians 3:16)
9. Inseparable from God's love (Romans 8:38)

I also want to direct your attention to a quote I used previously from John 17:20 (I've underlined a really important word):

> "...for those who <u>will</u> believe in me...I have given them the glory that you gave me..."

Think about that for a while. And then, consider this one:

> "But now he has reconciled you by Christ's physical body through death to present you holy in his sight, without blemish and free from accusation – if you continue in your faith..." (Colossians 1:22-23a).

Now, go back and read it more closely. He says that you are holy in His sight. Not trash, not nothing, not junk – holy. And, there is much more...*much* more. The OLD you – the one who dies when you find salvation – that OLD you is dead and forever gone. It's time to move on from lamentations and righteous suffering to celebrating victory. It's done. Jesus told the Jewish leaders:

> *"...you accept glory from one another but do not seek the glory that comes from the only God?" (John 5:44).*

It's time to seek the glory that comes from the only God. Not for ourselves do we seek this glory – we seek it for the One – the Son – the Holy One of Israel – the Word. And, we'll get it. Count on it, because Heaven can hardly wait.

Chapter 17 – Your Work Life

Do not let the people you work with define how you feel about your job or your work environment. There is an abundance of clueless, direction-less, lost souls out there, who want you to join them in their lost-ness. It makes them feel better if someone next to them is equally lost – it *is* the fallen human nature that drives this. Note that I said human nature, and not God nature. God isn't lost and never will be. Also, don't forget that it's part of your job as God's child to feed clues to them. Meanwhile, you are to be content with where you are. Out in the desert, John the Baptist was asked by a group of soldiers, "What should we do?"

> *"He replied, 'Don't extort money and don't accuse people falsely - be content with your pay'" (Luke 3:14).*

It doesn't say that you should not try to improve your knowledge and skills, thus becoming worth more in the marketplace. It says to be content – now – not someday, later, when the world is rosy with sunshine, lollipops and rainbows. You can be content while taking night classes, or studying on weekends.

> *"I am not saying this because I am in need, for I have learned to be content whatever the circumstances" (Philippians 4:11).*

The Alpha Male

Be forewarned – if you encourage someone who is stuck in whine-mode, they may increase their volume to deny that moment of blessing. You can't make anyone receive a blessing. But, you're supposed to be working for the Lord, not man. Bless them, anyway. Don't forget to smile.

> *"Whatever you do, work at it with all your heart, as working for the Lord, not for human masters, since you know that you will receive an inheritance from the Lord as a reward. It is the Lord Christ you are serving" (Colossians 3:23-24).*

Complaining

Complaining is poison. It's an internal poison of the heart that makes you open your mouth in order for it to come out. Remember the *"overflow, or abundance, of the heart?"* That's what the mouth is going to release. When grumbling, complaining, and blaming are the words spoken in your workplace, it poisons the workplace and those in it. Speaking death brings curses upon your workplace. If, as most people do, you spend a lot of your time at your place of work, then you may be exposed to curses that try to bring death or damage to your workplace. Speak life. Speak life to your workplace, to your fellow employees, to your manager, to those who report to your authority – speak life. You bring honor to the Lord when you work well – with diligence and respect. You are an example to those around you to work cheerfully and diligently. Your lifestyle is a constant reminder to those around you of who your Daddy is. Make Him proud. Joseph's inconveniences and trials became the pathway through which the Lord saved the twelve tribes of Israel from famine. Joseph had a very tough job with few rewards and plenty of trouble. He didn't complain. Instead, he pressed ahead and the Lord made him the administrator of the entire country.

Complaining is a declaration that circumstances are stronger and bigger than you. It declares that they are bigger and stronger than your God. It declares that you are **not** the Alpha Male. That's not what we're looking for here. We're building the man, not picking him apart, piece by piece. Every time your mouth opens to declare your lack of power and your helplessness, instead speak God's promises. Speak His authority. Speak His blessings. Live in it. Walk in it. It will change your life, forever.

> *"Do not let any unwholesome talk come out of your mouths, but only what is helpful for building others up according to their needs, that it may benefit those who listen" (Ephesians 4:29).*

Speak God's favor in your life. When your mouth opens, the world will hear of your provision and your every need being met in Glory, your soul prospering, your mind and your body prospering. You're a son of the King. He wants you to do well. Every father wants his children to do well. He wants you to prosper and extend His reign through your words and actions. He owns the universe, but He has given you dominion over this earth. His heart's desire is that your love for Him will lead you to bring His reign to this earth. It starts in your heart and comes out of your mouth.

> *"But if I drive out demons by the finger of God, then the kingdom of God has come upon you" (Luke 11:20).*

Drive the complaining and curses from your workplace with God's Word, so that His Kingdom comes upon your workplace. He gave you the authority – use it. Use your faith.

Every Alpha Male rules over territory. That territory grows or diminishes, based on a number of factors that are going on in your life during any given season. There are seasons when your focus is more inwardly-directed, such as when you have very small children. But when your life is ready for expansion, the Father is happy to expand your rule and reign if you're operating in it correctly. He wants you to be faithful in "the little" so that He can increase your scope of authority into "the big."

> "His master replied, 'Well done, good and faithful servant! You have been faithful with a few things; I will put you in charge of many things. Come and share your master's happiness!'" (Matthew 25:21).

In taking dominion and authority over your life and the territory God has given you, you declare your love and respect for the Father that brings Him honor like nothing else in this world. Honor God.

Beware of the Pack Mentality

There is Pack Mentality and Herd Mentality. Pack Mentality is a focused direction of energy, while Herd Mentality can be wandering and even aimless – it has no planned direction except to follow the herd. The Pack Mentality has a strong plan, and it's not necessarily a good one. Alpha Males, by their very nature will attract immature, less powerful, less authoritative individuals, who likely don't understand the manner in which one becomes an Alpha Male. It goes with the territory. You have to decide what type of relationship these individuals are looking for in order to determine whether to let the relationship proceed and grow or not, based on that determination. If the relationship is healthy and you are attracting men who are curious and want to know more about what you're doing, then you have a perfect opportunity to be a mentor – pointing them to the Lord and His plan. No one has to continue to act like the mythical Beta Male. The Lord intends that every man will become the Alpha Male. But, the

John H. Ingle

Pack Mentality leads to potentially dangerous situations. Packs of dogs, two or more is all that's required, can be dangerous, doing things that none of them would do by themselves. If you don't understand what I mean, watch some online videos about crowds and animals going out of control. Crowds can take an ugly turn very quickly. There is a dangerous pack mentality that takes over as people respond to their baser, primitive selves, abandoning the restraints that our minds normally place on us due to our morals, social membership and conditioning. Some social conditioning is a good thing, done properly. It shows us the fencelines and bar ditches, and we learn to stay out of them.

In more subtle situations, the pack mentality can be a serious impediment to your growth. In a job environment, the pack can be an ugly, demotivating, and even destructive force. Negativity is a cancer in any environment, including the job environment. People in groups have the opportunity to combine their strength and their mental faculties for good or for evil. Once that combined force is activated, it's very difficult to stop. I read recently of a toddler that had accidentally fallen into an African dog exhibit at a zoo. He was mangled and killed, immediately. The pack mentality is so strong, that even though these dogs were well fed and cared for, they went into kill-mode the moment an opportunity arrived. It was immediate and deadly.

People who are misguided or weak-willed can all-too-easily fall victim to the pack mentality, and turn their thinking over to someone else. I'm convinced that much of the horror of the Nazi regime in World War II was a perfect example of pack mode thinking. You can see what happens when men turn their decision-making process over to someone they see as powerful and god-like in their authority. The end result was sixty-million dead people. That's powerful alright –

The Alpha Male

powerful and nauseatingly awful on a scale that the mind cannot even fathom. Very often you can see the results of investment decisions that are made in the financial markets that are driven by pack, or herd, mentality. Financial bubbles are the result of too many people (the herd) chasing after too little an opportunity. Usually it will be a stampede started by the pack, to take advantage of the ignorance of the herd. The Pack Mentality can ruin a local Church body from the inside. Beware of the Pack Mentality.

Working the Night Shift

Circadian rhythms are essentially your twenty-four hour clock and its alignment with sunshine and nighttime. For many, many thousands of years, when the sun went down, you could burn a fire or go to bed. Modern man has decided that a 24 hour clock should be running for 24 hours – there's always something to do or some bizarre schedule to work. As it turns out, there is also a relationship between the hormone cortisol that we talked about earlier, and your circadian rhythms. That story is too complicated to be told here, but reading up on that topic would probably be valuable to you if you work the nightshift. But, another related story is how phone and computer screens are messing with our circadian rhythms, at our peril.

Harvard Medical School has been involved with studies showing that light containing high levels in the blue spectrum can disrupt and shift our circadian rhythms. It also suppresses the natural production of melatonin produced in the brain that helps you fall asleep and stay asleep.

> *"The researchers put 10 people on a schedule that gradually shifted the timing of their circadian rhythms. Their blood sugar levels increased, throwing them into a prediabetic state, and*

levels of leptin, a hormone that leaves people feeling full after a meal, went down... Light at night is part of the reason so many people don't get enough sleep...and researchers have linked short sleep to increased risk for depression, as well as diabetes and cardiovascular problems."

This is really important for those working night shifts. It also means that if you stay up late playing computer games you're likely not getting good quality sleep and consequently need more than normal and still feel tired. LED lighting typically produces much more light in the blue spectrum than did the incandescent bulb that has been largely outlawed. The LED is very power efficient but we may need to be more careful about how we use it. Manufacturers are becoming more aware of the issue and many of them are providing color balance mechanisms that allow you to restrict the amount of blue light on your electronic device screens. One of the new popular computer operating systems has a setting in the Display app that lets you set a time of day when the screen shifts into reduced blue spectrum. It's a seemingly small issue, but can work in tandem in your body to collect with other factors into a bigger issue that isn't easily traceable to a specific cause.

Chapter 18 – Habits

> *"It was the precocious Russian anthropologist Lev Semenovich Vygotsky who pointed out in the 1920's that to describe an isolated human mind is to miss the point. Human minds are never isolated. More than those of any other species, they swim in a sea called culture."* (Matt Ridley, in *Nature via Nurture*).

Alpha Males face many challenges in today's world. Some challenges are big and loud. Others hide in the weeds and we hardly see them. All too often we tend to live inside our heads, barely able to share the world we think we know. Like an old, well-worn shoe that we know so well, our world, to someone else, can look just like that old shoe. It isn't something they even want to touch, much less try on. That highly personal world is filled with habits. Habits drive a very large part of our daily activities in life. When you're not deliberately in charge of your actions or thoughts, your habits and routines are driving for you. You might be surprised what a high percentage of our average day is in habit-drive. We need activities and goals in our lives that keep snapping us out of our sleep-walking contentment. Immersing yourself in God's word is one of those activities. Remember that there is no autopilot and briefly recall and visualize that mountainside in the clouds I mentioned earlier in this book.

What is it that makes us amnesia victims on a regular basis? How is it that I can get up each morning and it takes me a while to get my bearings and invite God into my day with me? I have had many days when I would arrive at work and be confronted with a three alarm fire (according to a client or co-worker) and hours later realize that I hadn't invited the Lord God to join me and to feel free to make suggestions. Point to remember: always invite the Lord to make suggestions.

Habits – Making Them and Breaking Them

Making new, constructive, rewarding habits is harder than it sounds. If you watch people around New Year's you can see a whole cottage industry spring up around resolutions touting "new behaviors" and "new lifestyles." Gyms prepare to sign up a whole new crop of members that likely will not be showing up very often after mid-February. In the world of magazines, Cosmo can tell you the ten latest rumors about how to improve your sex life but can't help you deal with serious issues of the mind and spirit. The internet is quite handy for how-to videos for your lawnmower and quickie facts about the number of registered voters in Philadelphia. But, it is an echo chamber for serious information about how our minds and bodies work. Out on the web, quackery abounds.

One particular popular "fact" is that you can make or break a habit in twenty-one days. It has spread like a scandalous rumor throughout the internet where you can find the twenty-one day figure repeated and quoted over and over, again. Often, it's circular quoting as they use each other's quotes to reinforce and support their own, without anyone being able to account for where it originally came from. It is unfortunate that this timeframe has become the benchmark for the expectation of self-improvement in the world of habits. So many people, Christians included, become disheartened by not being able to fix their problems in twenty-one days. After all, the magazine article said that's all it takes. Their opinion of themselves can end up worse than when they started. Failure here can become the freshly sown seed of a bad conscience, and we find ourselves not wanting to try facing that unsuccessful personal challenge, again. We doubt ourselves and then find concurring testimony in that recent failure – that we're weak and unable to change. The accuser is always ready to help you condemn yourself.

The scientific world has a very different opinion regarding habits (automaticity) and what it really takes to make and break them. In an online article from the National Institute of Health, real scientists like Benjamin Gardner, Phillippa Lally, and Jane Wardle give us a very different view. Their article, originally published in the British Journal of General Practice, has this to say regarding the twenty-one day rumor:

> "This myth appears to have originated from anecdotal evidence of patients who had received plastic surgery treatment and typically adjusted psychologically to their new appearance within 21 days."

Looking closely at the time it really takes to modify our entrenched behavior patterns, they have this to offer:

> "...automaticity plateaued on average around 66 days after the first daily performance, although there was considerable variation across participants and behaviours. Therefore, it may be helpful to tell patients to expect habit formation (based on daily repetition) to take around 10 weeks."

That's *ten* weeks instead of *three*. And, in a separate study that Lally took part in, she notes that it sometimes takes much longer to completely break a habit – somewhere between 18 and 254 days. The truth is that some habits take very careful work to cultivate. Breaking or modifying those habits may take an equal or greater amount of work. Making a habit that has the reward of fame, fortune or pleasure can be somewhat easier, even if those rewards are only fleeting or imaginary. Breaking a negative habit is often accompanied by some sort of negative feedback from our environment – the feeling of "doing without" or "deprivation," which can make it more difficult to stay the course. Breaking it could also take the form of physical or emotional pain, or some imagined loss of social stature. Breaking a negative habit often leads to some sort of substitution with a replacement activity, which can be another new problem that we just don't see or understand, yet.

If you decide to learn more about habits, find your way to actual scientific studies and bypass the self-help sites that mostly regurgitate the most recent un-researched rumor. In the meantime, know that removing a bad habit works out a lot better when we pray about it frequently and seek other, more positive behavior to replace it. Years ago, I was a smoker. I tried numerous times to quit and stay quit, but it kept coming back like the memory of a bad car wreck that happened last week. Finally, one late night, the Lord told me, "If you don't quit you will die from it." Okay, that's it. I'm done. I didn't go back after that. I was immediately cured. I suppose sometimes we are just so entrenched in a bad behavior that it takes a serious spiritual intervention to get the job done. My hope for you is that you'll be successful much more quickly than I was.

The most unhappy a man can be is with himself. Within that self-dissatisfaction lurks the condemnation and loss of heart that causes him to seek addictions and destructions – the judgment to destroy himself. We are taught not to judge. We should observe that concept for our own lives – seeking God's perfect vision rather than finding ourselves less than perfect and continually condemning ourselves for being that way. It contradicts God – you are fearfully and wonderfully made. You were built to operate in freedom, not in the bondage of the accumulation of habits you acquire over the years. Equally as true, if you operate under the bondage of your past or the opinions of others, then you won't be fully free to live and function as a son or daughter of the Most High.

> *"It is for freedom that Christ has set us free. Stand firm, then, and do not let yourselves be burdened again by a yoke of slavery... You, my brothers and sisters, were called to be free. But do not use your freedom to indulge the flesh; rather, serve one another humbly in love"* (Galatians 5:1,13).

Habits That Help Build the Man

When cleaning out old, negative habits, add some good ones to fill your time and thoughts. Being in the Word, every day, is a great way to strengthen both your resolve and your relationship with the Lord. I try to read my Bible every morning (at least) – not because I think I'm racking up holiness points on some scoreboard in Heaven – but because the Lord uses that activity to speak to me. On numerous occasions I have needed to hear a word or counsel on a specific question or problem, and have gotten exactly what I needed through a morning Bible session.

As an example, in June 2005 it appeared that I might need to officiate at a wedding ceremony and did not have the ministerial documents to allow me to legally do that. I went online and located a program through which I could obtain a certificate declaring me an Independent Christian Clergy that would allow me to legally preside over the ceremony. It wasn't just a fee-for-paper situation – there were things I had to do to "qualify." But, I was concerned about the perception that this might leave with some people – sort of a "degree online" and now I'm a PhD. I didn't want it to be cheesy, or subject to ridicule in the eyes of man. I asked the Lord to make it real – to make it something that He would be proud for me to do – something that would represent the big changes the Lord had been making in my life over the years. He said, "Acts 4:10." That's all, just a Bible verse. He's often very specific. I went to my Bible and found:

> "...then know this, you and all the people of Israel: It is by the name of Jesus Christ of Nazareth, whom you crucified but whom God raised from the dead, that this man stands before you healed."

There it was – God's testimony, not mine – I was the man healed. I had no more lingering doubts about where I stood with God. As far as He was concerned, that was old news, and now it's time to do something new. God doesn't worry about your past; He's concerned about your future.

In the early days of writing this book, I picked up my Bible one morning and asked the Lord for something to help me nail this whole idea of the Alpha Male and what it means. As I opened my Bible and began to read, I saw:

> "I give you thanks with all my heart. Not to idols, but to you I sing praise. I bow down toward your holy temple and give thanks to your name for your grace and truth; for you have made your word [even] greater than the whole of your reputation. When I called, you answered me, you made me bold and strong" (Psalm 138:1-3 CJB).

The Alpha Male

It was as if the very last line was coming through a big outdoor concert sound system and my eyes stuck firmly on the phrase "bold and strong," and I couldn't look away. It was exactly what I was looking for – the succinct statement of what it means to be the Alpha Male. I like the original Hebrew even better – bold and stout of heart – stouthearted. The word stouthearted conveys more of a mental picture and is in keeping with the essence of Hebrew. A few weeks later I went to the Lord before my Bible reading time, feeling a little down, a little lethargic, looking for a pep talk from the Lord. Life wasn't being so easy and comfy – things weren't just falling into place for me. He said, *"Open your Bible to the middle and back up two pages. Put your finger down, and read."* I opened my Bible to what looked like the middle and turned back two pages. My finger and eye fell straight to the verses that read:

> *"I give you thanks with all my heart...When I called, you answered me, you made me bold and strong."*

That was about as good an answer to my need as I was ever going to get – *"I give you thanks with all my heart"* and he made me *"bold and strong."* All that was necessary was that <u>I believe Him</u> – *use my faith* – and walk out the life that He intends for me to live – living bold and strong, all the while praising Him. Yep – that would be the Alpha Male. It sounded a lot like Daniel in the lion's den – not fearful, but brave and resolute, knowing that the Lord had authority over the lions and that his job was to stand there – bold and strong, awaiting the King's return. It also reminded me of David, walking out to meet Goliath, not fearful, but brave and resolute.

Willfulness

If there is an Achilles heel for the Alpha Male it is willfulness – that streak of impulse that tells us that we have figured it out and we'll take care of this one, ourselves. I am living proof of that. Willfulness is a disconnection. God calls it "quenching the Spirit." Do you really want to hang up on God while He's talking to you? No, you don't. Yet, we do it often, under the guise of independence, or self-reliance. We pretty it up like a gaudy commercial that has too much flashing of lights and too many loud noises. We do that to cover over the fact that we just ducked out of the phone call and don't want to hear His opinion on the matter.

You might think that willfulness is a result of pride – they are very closely connected. I tend to see them as chicken and egg, but not the same thing. Willfulness is what you see when a small child says, "I do it," when a sibling or parent is doing something with them and the child wants control. It's an impulse. Pride comes when the impulse yields fruit and the child sees it as a result of their authority over the situation. They see themselves become master of it, and find pleasure in the feeling. It's a dangerous moment for a man and recalls the verse:

> *"For everything in the world—the lust of the flesh, the lust of the eyes, and the pride of life—comes not from the Father but from the world" (1 John 2:16).*

The pride of life is that lusty moment when we look out at the world and feel like conquerors – winners taking all in a raw contest of brains and muscle – victors gathering our spoils. Again, there is that temptation – stepping into the same trap that felled Satan – the pride of life, lusting to be in charge of the universe. Abraham Lincoln said:

The Alpha Male

"Nearly all men can stand adversity, but if you want to test a man's character, give him power."

I would add to that, "riches." The combination of riches and power are a drink so powerful that it can turn unprepared men into lusting drunkards in a heartbeat. Western civilization seems to be judging itself and has pronounced a guilty verdict on mankind that demands justice. The problem is that the justice it appears to want requires death to the guilty – self destruction – not salvation through Jesus. Western civilization, itself, is being drawn down pathways that lead only to death. The value of human life teeters at the brink.

Chapter 19 – Traveling in the Wake of Our Fathers

What Have We Learned?

1. Real women want real men. Real women want an Alpha Male.
2. Alpha Males want a real Bride.
3. It takes a real woman to be the Bride of an Alpha Male.
4. God intends that every family is led by an Alpha Male.
5. The Alpha Male longs to hear the Father's voice in all matters.
6. The Alpha Male lives in the spirit – from Heaven towards Earth.
7. The Alpha Male seeks wisdom and truth as uncountable riches.
8. The Alpha Male teaches and prepares his family as part of the Bride of Christ.
9. The assault on the Alpha Male by the world culture is intensifying and isn't going to stop until time stops.
10. The Church (body of Christ) is the primary source of true Alpha Males.
11. The modern culture has invaded the Church body with teachings that undermine and misinterpret the Holy Spirit and produce weak churches inhabited by weak Christians.

12. The weakened Church has been churning out seed that don't produce fruit. The seed have no roots and wither in the onslaught of evil. The result is a severe shortage of Alpha Males and families that don't survive or thrive.
13. The shortage of Alpha Males is causing women to think they must assume the role. The role doesn't fit how God made them and real Alpha Males are not attracted to them.
14. The Church needs to get back to doing its job, which is to produce Alpha Males and Brides that build and grow families whose desire is to serve the Lord and carry the Gospel to all nations.
15. There are more stones coming.

Standing on Their Shoulders

Our father's ceiling is our floor. The things that are important in life – the things that you pour yourself into – the things you would live and die for, are the things that you will long to pass on to your kids. Our fathers and the fathers of the Church have put more than we can imagine into what we've been given in this life. Find those things that were important in your fathers' lives that are important to you and important to God. Take for yourself those things that have been gained, and use them to build your own legacy that you will pass to your children. Tell them that you're doing it. Show them what you're doing and why. Help them build an appreciation for what has come before them.

Fresh Wind

Fresh wind is a sailing term that describes that new breeze that suddenly billows and then fills the sails, the telltales sewn to the sail flicker and stand, and the boat seems almost to leap forward with new energy and excitement. When that happens in our spirit, God's Holy Spirit is in His rightful place in our life. Pray for that fresh wind in your heart and that leaping forward to new things that God has waiting for each of us. Unplug regularly and get close to the outdoors; not as conquerors but as citizens of it. Your body was designed and created by God to act in harmony with this big ball we live on. Feel the sun and wind, and even the rain to reconnect with what God designed for you to live in.

The Alpha Male is not on his knees worshipping the golden calf. The golden calf is a representation of man resorting to his own devices, alone in the universe with no prospect for more than the here-and-now, casting about for some omen or lucky break. Not only is there no prospect for "more than this" without God, but there's still a judgment day coming for each of us to account for that which we've been entrusted. Jesus tells us the story of the talents and how they were used for the profit of the Master, or left, fruitless, producing nothing for the one who made the investment.

The primacy of God's love and goodness are vital to our understanding of our relationship with Him. His wrath is not the key. His judgment is not the key. Hell is not the key. Death is not the key. His love is the key. His love is the key to everything else – forgiveness, resurrection, atonement, blessings, gifts – ALL of His provision – not just the parts that promise to provide escape from the coming wrath.

You want to be the new wineskin of which Jesus spoke, ready to receive that new fullness of the Spirit spoken about by the Apostles. How else will the Church body get to "greater works than these?" The Alpha Male is galvanized and animated by the Holy Spirit, whether it is work or play, praying or eating, or even in being physically intimate with your wife. There is always a war going on for your heart – for

The Alpha Male

your point of view – for your world perspective. The Alpha Male is a warrior on the front lines of that war. The sign of rank on his collar or sleeve is not relevant – it doesn't matter. David had no rank at all when he slew Goliath. His brothers considered him a rank amateur, but God saw him differently. What God thinks about you is what matters.

Some of this book is what God said. The rest is what I've said. My goal is not to make you believe everything I tell you. My goal is for you to hear what I'm saying, and take the parts that seem to apply to your own life and ask God, "Is this truth and will it help me?" The history of the ages is that mortal men who've made great discoveries and said marvelous things have always had some ingredient or thought that was misled or corrupted through some element of their experience. But, I can still take what they said to God, and ask, "Is this truth?" And, I can know that there are things that are true, but that are superseded by higher "truth." And, the wonderful part about that question, when we ask it, is that God will answer me and you. He may not do it directly – he may direct your attention to a flock of dove, or to vividly recall a memory from childhood, or any number of vastly (seemingly) disconnected responses that He might summon from within us. God wants that conversation with you. It is His delight that you come to Him to talk about the important things – the things that make life, that cause us to experience love, compassion, and His presence. If you discover His delight, you will, in turn, discover your own. And, your own rests in Him. You will come full circle, back to the Author and Finisher of your faith, where you belonged, all the while. God is not hiding in a secret building somewhere, daring you to try and find Him like a too-well-hidden Easter egg. He's waiting for you to find *life* like an Easter egg. And, like any good Daddy, He always puts it somewhere you can find it. But, you have to look for it.

It is the *"Glory of God to conceal a matter..."* He wants to be worth your effort to look for Him.

> *"And, afterward, I will pour out my Spirit on all people. Your sons and daughters will prophesy, your old men will dream dreams, your young men will see visions. Even on my servants, both men and women, I will pour out my Spirit in those days" (Joel 2:28-29a).*

Let it rain, Lord.

Oh, and remember that He asked you to call Him "Daddy."

Selected Bibliography

This bibliography is by no means a complete record of all the resources used to produce this book. I list these sources as a convenience for those who wish to pursue certain subjects in greater detail.

Benner, Jeff, American Hebrew Research Center: https://www.youtube.com/watch?v=8-a52NxLuVQ&index=26&list=PL8z4SxaOFThRONsuKBxTrgM1zRfuGtNbw

Benner, Jeff - https://www.ancient-hebrew.org/ahlb/index.html

Bible Gateway Website, https://www.biblegateway.com

Bivins, David, Roy Blizzard Jr., *Understanding the Difficult Words of Jesus*, Shippensburg, PA, Destiny Image, 1994.

Blizzard, Roy III, https://hubpages.com/religion-philosophy/Are-Jesus-and-God-One, *Are Jesus and God One?* 2013.

Brown, Francis, S.R. Driver, Charles A. Briggs, *The Brown-Driver-Briggs Hebrew and English Lexicon*, Peabody, MA, Hendrickson Publishers, 2003.

Gardner, Benjamin, Phillippa Lally, Jane Wardle, *Making health habitual: the psychology of 'habit-formation' and general practice,* htttps://www.ncbi.nlm.nih.gov/pmc/articles/PMC3505409/, British Journal of General Practice, Dec. 2012, DOI: 10.3399/bjgp12X659466.

Harvard Medical School, Harvard Health Publishing, *Blue Light Has a Dark Side*, https://www.health.harvard.edu/staying-healthy/blue-light-has-a-dark-side, May 2012, Updated August 2018.

Higgins, Agnes, Michael Nash, Aileen M. Lynch, *Antidepressant-associated sexual dysfunction: impact, effects, and treatment*. https://www.ncbi.nlm.nih.gov/pmc/articles/PMC3108697/. September 9, 2010.

Lally, Phillippa, Cornelia H. M. Van Jaarsveld, Henry W. W. Potts, Jane Wardle, *How are habits formed: Modelling habit formation in the real world*, European Journal of Social Psychology 40, 998–1009 (2010), Published online 16 July 2009 in Wiley Online Library, (wileyonlinelibrary.com) DOI: 10.1002/ejsp.674 University College London, London, UK

Tyrrell, Mark, Roger Elliot, *Side Effects of Antidepressants*, https://www.clinical-depression.co.uk/dlp/treating-depression/side-effects-of-antidepressants/

Various Hebrew Translations, http://www.qbible.com/hebrew-old-testament/

Made in the USA
Coppell, TX
26 October 2019